CONCISE DICTIONARY OF NATURE

Grafton Books
A Division of the Collins Publishing Group
8 Grafton Street, London W1X 3LA

Published by Grafton Books 1986
Copyright © Grafton Books 1986

British Library Cataloguing in Publication Data
Dictionary of nature.—(Pocket dictionaries)
  1. Biology
  I. Glassborow, Jilly. II. Series
  574   QH307.2

  ISBN 0–246–12731–7

Printed in Great Britain by
Hazell Watson & Viney Ltd, Aylesbury

CONCISE
DICTIONARY
OF NATURE

edited by
JILLY GLASSBOROW

GRAFTON BOOKS

A Division of the Collins Publishing Group

LONDON GLASGOW
TORONTO SYDNEY AUCKLAND

A

Aaron's rod See MULLEIN.

Abalone See ORMER.

Abdomen In arthropods – the hind portion of the body, as distinct from the head and thorax, consisting of several similar segments. In mammals – the part of the body containing the intestines, liver and kidneys.

Acacia, false See LOCUST TREE.

Acclimatization Changes in an animal or plant that take place in response to a change in environment (e.g. temperature, location, light) and which enable the organism to survive under the new conditions, though not necessarily to reproduce.

Aconite, winter A low flowering plant with yellow blooms, belonging to the buttercup family. It is found mainly in gardens.

Acorn The fruit of an oak tree.

Acorns

Acorn-shell See BARNACLE.

Adam and Eve See LORDS AND LADIES.

Adaptation Changes in a plant or animal that increase the organism's ability to survive and reproduce in a given environment. Such changes may develop over many generations before an organism is fully adapted to its environment.

Adder Also called the common viper, this poisonous snake is found throughout Europe except in the extreme south and Ireland. It grows to about 65 cm long and is

Adder

characterized by the dark zig-zag markings along its grey or brown back. It also has vertical pupils in its eyes, unlike all other NW European snakes, which have round pupils. Adders give birth to live young enclosed in a thin membrane.

Aestivation (1) The arrangement of petals in a flower bud before the bud opens out. (2) A period of dormancy undertaken by some animals during the summer to avoid the harmful effects of high temperatures and lack of water. Certain snails and amphibians aestivate.

Agaric, fly A colourful and poisonous toadstool commonly found under birch and pine trees. The cap is bright red with white 'warts', although these are often missing in older specimens. With age the cap becomes saucer-shaped and may fade to orange.

Agrimony Two species of flowering plant related to the rose and found mainly in dry grassy areas. Their yellow flowers are arranged to form a thin spike. The unrelated hemp agrimony belongs to the daisy family and is tall with clusters of pink flowers.

Albino An animal that lacks skin pigments, resulting in a pure white individual. The pink eyes associated with albinism are due to the lack of pigment in the iris which allows the colour of the blood show through.

Alder Member of a group of deciduous trees, belonging to the

Alder trees

birch family, that thrive in wet places. The trees grow about 25 metres tall. The flowers are arranged as catkins and open before the leaves. The female catkins are woody and barrel-shaped. The common alder has dark, almost black bark and rounded leaves. The grey alder has grey bark and toothed triangular leaves.

Alder fly A group of insects with long antennae and two pairs of large wings. The eggs, laid near water, hatch into swimming larvae that feed on small insects and worms. The dark brown adult grows up to 30 mm long and is a poor flier. It rests by day near water, often in alder trees.

Alexanders A tall early-flowering plant of the carrot family which produces clusters of small yellow flowers and has glossy leaves. It is found mainly in hedgerows and on wastelands near the coast.

Alga A group of simple plants, most of which live in water, others in damp places on land. About 25,000 different kinds are known, some green, some brown and some red. Many are single-celled, and too small to be seen without a microscope. Others are large seaweeds. Algae can make food from sunlight by the process called photosynthesis, and in turn provide food for animals.

Alkanet Several species of mainly blue-flowered plant with hairy leaves and stems, belonging to the borage family. The green alkanet has leafy clusters of blue flowers on long stalks. It is often found in woods and hedgerows.

Almond A deciduous tree of south-western Asia which has been grown in Europe for many hundreds of

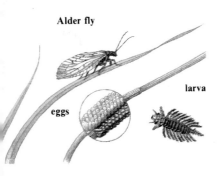

Alder fly

larva

eggs

Wild almond

years. It belongs to the rose family. There are several varieties of almond which can be divided into two groups – those producing sweet, edible nuts and those with bitter nuts. The trees are grown in warmer southern parts for their nuts but in NW Europe they are grown for their pretty pink blossom.

Alternation of generations The regular occurrence of two distinct forms during the life cycle of an animal or plant. The best examples are seen among the ferns and their relatives. The mature fern scatters spores, but instead of growing into new fern plants the spores produce totally different plants known as prothalli. These are tiny green plates that grow unnoticed on the ground. Male and female cells are produced and fertilization takes place on the prothalli. The fertilized female cells grow into new fern plants.

Amoeba Tiny protozoan (one-celled organism) which can only be seen with a microscope. Amoebae are made of a jelly-like material called cytoplasm and have no fixed shape. An amoeba can move by pushing out part of the cytoplasm to make a 'false foot' or pseudopodium. By sending out several false feet it can encircle and trap food particles. Amoebae reproduce mainly by dividing into two.

Amphibian A cold-blooded animal belonging to the vertebrate class Amphibia which contains the frogs, newts and toads and salamanders. Some spend all their lives in water, and the others usually return to the water to breed. Most amphibians undergo metamorphosis during their development, hatching from the eggs as gill-breathing larvae called tadpoles. Most adults have lungs and scaleless moist skins through which they can breathe.

Amphioxus See LANCELET.

Amphipods

Amphipod A group of small, shrimp-like crustaceans found in both salt and fresh water. Most have bodies flattened from side to side and move on land by jumping. The sand hoppers seen jumping about in the seaweed on beaches are a common example.

Anchovy A small marine fish, only 14 cm long, related to the herring. It lives in large shoals in estuaries or shallow bays, particularly in the Mediterranean, but goes to deeper water in winter. Before the Dutch Zuider Zee (now the IJsselmeer) was dammed and partly reclaimed it was a rich source of anchovies.

Anchovy

Anemone Several species of flowering plant related to the buttercup and often known as windflowers. The most common is the wood anemone which forms a thick white carpet in woodlands. Its leaves are arranged in a whorl beneath the solitary flower. The short-stalked yellow anemone and the blue anemone may also be found in woodlands.

Angelica, wild A tall herb belonging to the carrot family and found mainly in fens and woods. The grooved stem supports clusters of small white or pink flowers. The sweet angelica used in cooking comes from the stems of the closely related garden angelica which bears yellow-green flowers.

Angiosperm A large group of plants which produce flowers and bear their seeds in fruits.

Anglerfish A bottom-living fish with an enormous head and huge jaws. There is a long fin-ray on the top of its head which the fish waves about to lure other fishes into its jaws. Up to about 170 cm long, the anglerfish can catch quite large prey, and has even been known to snap up diving birds.

Angle shade A common European moth which at rest looks like a dead leaf. It flies all year round. The caterpillar is green or brown, with V-shaped markings on the back, and feeds on a variety of green plants.

Angle shade

Animal kingdom One of the two divisions of all living things, loosely defined as comprising those organisms which move about freely and feed on plants or other animals. There is no mistaking the kingdom (plant or animal) to which the more advanced animals belong. But there is a grey area among primitive creatures, particularly the single-celled protozoa, where it is difficult to define an organism as being wholly animal or plant. The diagram on page 190 shows the most generally accepted division.

Annelid Member of a group of soft-bodied worms with long, distinctly ringed or segmented bodies. Annelids are protected by a tough outer coat and some are coated with bristles. Some are hermaphrodite and many are able to regenerate missing parts. The group includes the earthworms, bristleworms and leeches.

Annual A plant that completes its life cycle in one year – growing from seed to mature plant, producing seeds and dying.

Annual ring One of a series of concentric lines found in tree trunks growing in temperate climates. Each ring represents a year's growth. This is because growth is not constant throughout the year and the woody elements produced during spring are very much larger than those of the late summer, just before growth stops. The later growth is therefore more compact and appears as a darker ring.

Ant About 15,000 species of social insect, related to bees and wasps. Ants live in large colonies and are easily recognizable by their slim 'waists', large heads and bent antennae. In a typical ant colony, the queen lays eggs which are tended by numerous wingless females called

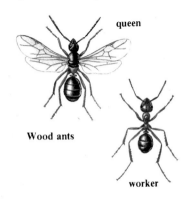

queen

Wood ants

worker

Ant lion

larva

workers. In some species, there are large workers called soldiers; they have extra-large jaws and their task is to defend the nest or simply to crush hard foods. None of the workers lays eggs. Every year some of the eggs produce new queens and winged males, which mate during a 'wedding flight' from the nest. Afterwards the males die, but the queens either remain to increase the size of the existing nest or go off to found new colonies. Many ants live on other insects but their diet is varied. Some 'milk' aphids for their honey-dew.

Antenna Sensory appendage on the head of many arthropods, i.e. insects, crustaceans, and millipedes and centipedes. Antennae grow in pairs and are often long and mobile with many joints.

Anther See STAMEN.

Antler Bony growth from the skull of deer, usually branched and initially covered in fine skin called velvet. Antlers grow in pairs and are shed each year. Each year's antlers are larger than those of the year before, until the animal reaches maturity. After this they remain the same size for a few years, and then may actually decline. Except in the case of reindeer, antlers are confined to the males.

Ant lion A group of insects which look like dragonflies but are distinguished by their clubbed antennae. They are mainly nocturnal and catch small flies and other insects. The larvae of most species are free-living in soil and leaf litter,

but some dig pits in which they hide, waiting for ants and other insects to fall in. Such strong predatory instincts give the ant lion its name. Most species live in southern Europe but one is found as far north as Finland.

Aphid A group of tiny insects that includes greenfly and blackfly. Aphids are bugs, and are also known as plant lice. They are serious pests to farmers and gardeners as they deform plants by sucking their sap. They also spread plant diseases. Aphids may be tended by ants, which 'milk' them for the sweet honey-dew they produce.

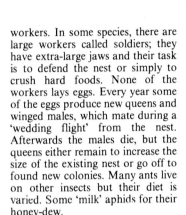

Rose aphids

Apollo

Ash, common A tall deciduous tree, up to 40 metres high, belonging to the olive family. It has pale grey bark, and is easily recognizable in winter by its black buds. The small purple male and female flowers usually grow on separate trees and open before the leaves. The winged seeds hang in bunches and are called keys. The mountain ash is an unrelated species of tree, also known as ROWAN.

Common ash

Apollo A medium-sized butterfly found on mountains in mainland Europe. There are several races, mostly with white, yellow or grey wings and dark markings. The large spots on the hind wing are usually red or orange.

Arachnid Member of the group of arthropods containing the spiders, harvestmen, scorpions and mites. Arachnids are most readily distinguished from insects by their four pairs of walking legs (an insect has three pairs). They have two pairs of appendages on the head: the first set are tiny pincers used for grasping and crushing prey, the second are palps used for grasping or sensing.

Arrow worm A group of long, transparent, worm-like animals that are abundant in marine plankton. They are most common in warm seas but a few species are found in the seas around NW Europe. Their bodies are often arrow-shaped and there are fins on the sides and tail.

Arthropod Member of a large group of invertebrates with segmented bodies and paired jointed legs. The body is protected by a hard outer coating made largely of chitin. The phylum Arthropoda contains the insects, crustaceans, arachnids, millipedes and centipedes, and is the largest in the animal kingdom.

Asp A freshwater fish, belonging to the carp family, that lives in central Europe. Asps are solitary fish. They grow up to 1 metre long and live in slow-running rivers.

Aspen

Puffin **Guillemot** **Razorbill** **Little auk**

Aspen A type of poplar, with rounded leaves held on long stalks, which quiver even on apparently still days. The male and female catkins grow on separate trees, as in all POPLARS.

Assassin bug A group of long-legged bugs which suck blood through a pointed 'beak'. They feed mainly on other insects but sometimes attack humans. Some assassin bugs are brightly coloured, but most are black or brown. They grow from 10 to 25 mm long.

Assassin-fly See ROBBER-FLY.

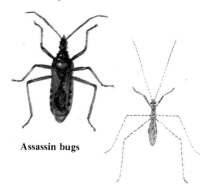

Assassin bugs

Auk A group of seabirds, including the little auk, PUFFIN, GUILLEMOT and RAZORBILL. They are black and white birds, with slim, stubby wings, just as at home in the sea as in the air. Auks nest on sea cliffs, and spend most of their time at sea, catching fish.

Avens Several species of flowering plant belonging to the rose family. The mountain avens is a low creeping plant with a long stem and solitary, small, white flowers. It is found on mountain rocks and on low ground in the north. The water avens is a plant of shady wet places and produces dull pink flowers.

Avocet An elegant white and black shorebird with long grey legs and a long, thin, black beak.

Axil Angle between the upper side of a leaf and the stem from which it grows.

Azalea, wild A colourful flowering plant related to the heather. It is a low creeping shrub which forms a mat of tiny pink flowers, and is commonly found high up on mountains and on Arctic heaths.

11

B

Backswimmer A group of true bugs which swim upside down in ponds and streams, using their back legs as 'oars'. They eat tadpoles and other water animals and can give a painful bite. When diving, backswimmers trap a bubble of air against their abdomen. They are sometimes called water boatmen, though the true water boatmen form a separate group.

Bacterium A single-celled organism usually classed as a plant and visible only through a microscope. Millions of bacteria are on everything we touch, including our own skin. They play an important part in breaking down dead matter in the soil, and are able to survive in places where no other living things can, for example, in hot springs. Bacteria multiply at an enormous rate by splitting into two every half hour or so. Some cause disease, while others are useful in medicine. Some bacteria are needed to make certain foods, including cheese.

Badger A thickset carnivore closely related to the weasel. It is about 70 cm long with coarse greyish fur and has a white head with broad black stripes running through the eyes on each side. The animal builds a large maze of underground tunnels, called a set, where it lives with its family, coming out at night to feed on worms, small mammals, fruit and nuts.

Bagworm moth A moth so named because its larva makes a 'bag' of silk interwoven with leaf and twig fragments, and carries this around. When the larva or bagworm is ready to pupate it attaches the case to a twig and pupates inside it. Female bagworm moths have neither wings nor legs, and they remain per-manently inside the larval case. The males do have wings and emerge in the early summer to fly by day.

Baleen Horny plates of the protein keratin which hang down from the upper jaw of toothless whales. Also known as whalebone. The whales filter water through the plates to catch the tiny crustaceans on which they feed.

Balm A white-flowered, lemon-scented herb used for cooking and often for medicine. It is of medium height with whorls of pointed oval leaves.

Himalayan balsam

Balsam A family of hairless plants with fleshy stems, easily recognized by their spurred, two-lipped flowers. One species is often called touch-me-not as the fruit bursts at the slightest touch. It has bright yellow flowers. The more common Himalayan or Indian balsam was introduced from Asia. It has large pink flowers and grows by fresh water.

Barbel (1) A freshwater fish belonging to the carp family, that gets its name from the four barbels on its

Badgers

upper lip. It lives in clear, fast-flowing stretches of rivers during the summer, and spends the winter hibernating in large shoals in deeper water. (2) A fleshy filament hanging from a fish's mouth.

Barberry A low spiny shrub with yellow flowers in drooping spikes. It produces bright red berries and is found in hedgerows and scrubland.

Bark beetle A family of beetles, also called engraver beetles, that carve intricate patterns of tunnels beneath the bark of trees. Both the adults and the larvae are borers. Besides damaging timber, bark beetles also carry fungus diseases, such as Dutch elm disease, which can weaken and kill trees.

Barnacle A group of crustaceans related to the crabs and lobsters. Barnacle larvae swim freely but the adults usually attach themselves by the head to rocks, ships' bottoms, and sometimes other animals. They are protected by chalky plates which close over the body when the animal is out of water. When under water, the plates open out and the barnacle stretches out its feathery legs which act as combs to trap food. The acorn barnacle, whose white cones are found all over rocks on the shore, is the commonest species.

Acorn barnacles

Barnacle goose This bird was so named because it was once thought to hatch from the goose barnacle (a small crustacean of the seashore). It is a mostly grey goose, with a black neck and white face. It breeds in the Arctic and flies south to winter in warmer regions, where it lives in saltmarshes and estuaries.

Barn owls

Barn owl A family of owls with heart-shaped faces. There are 10 species, of which only one is commonly found in Europe. Those living in the British Isles and south-western Europe have white breasts, while those further east are darker-breasted. They nest in barns, church towers and similar buildings and can sometimes be seen flying by day. They are also called white owls, or screech owls after their long, strangled cry.

Bartsia A short plant with spikes of two-lipped flowers. The most common species, the red bartsia, is often tinged purple with purple flowers. It is found on waste ground.

Basil, wild A faintly aromatic plant, found in dry grassland or among rocks, with whorls of pink flowers.

Basil-thyme

Serotine bat

Basil-thyme A low, sprawling, hairy plant with violet-blue flowers. The flowers have a small white patch on the lower lip which guides bees to the nectar. Basil-thyme is usually found in fields and meadows.

Basket star See BRITTLE STAR.

Basking shark At 15 metres this is the world's second biggest shark. It feeds by filtering plankton from water passed over a series of horny rakers situated in the gill chambers. The sharks live singly or in shoals of up to 250 individuals. They live mostly south of Iceland but visit European waters during the summer.

Bass A name given to several types of fishes, both marine and freshwater. The common sea-bass is a predatory fish which lives in small shoals off rocky shores. It grows up to 80 cm long. The freshwater large-mouthed black bass is a member of the sunperch family, that has been introduced into European rivers from North America.

Bat The only mammal capable of flight, although several other mammals can glide. The wings are formed by large folds of skin stretched across the animal's long fingers and attached to its limbs and body. Bats are nocturnal creatures and all the European species eat insects such as moths. They have extremely poor vision, though they are not blind, and navigate in the dark by sending out high-pitched sounds which bounce off nearby objects. The bats detect these echoes with their highly sensitive ears, using the information to determine where the objects are. In this way they can locate something as small as a moth. Bats in temperate climates hibernate during the winter, generally hanging upside-down in a dark, sheltered place. See DAUBENTON'S BAT, HORSE-SHOE BAT, LONG-EARED BAT, MOUSE-EARED BAT, NATTERER'S BAT, NOCTULE BAT, PIPISTRELLE and WHISKERED BAT.

Beak (1) Horny projection surrounding a bird's mouth. The shape and size of a beak is related to the type of food a bird eats. Birds of prey, for instance, have sharp hooked beaks which they use to tear at the flesh of their prey. Finches, on the other hand, have short stout beaks well adapted for crushing fruits and seeds. (2) Bugs and the octopus also have 'beaks'.

Bear A large carnivore with powerful limbs, large strong claws and a very short tail. The brown bear is

Europe's only resident species. It is about 2 metres long and has a thick brown coat. It eats a wide variety of both plant and animal food. Brown bears used to live all over Europe but now survive in only a few forested, mountainous areas.

Beaver Europe's largest rodent, over 80 cm long. After many years of being hunted, European beavers are now found only in Scandinavia, Poland, East Germany and on the River Rhône in France. A colony of the very similar Canadian beavers has been established in Finland. Beavers have a large flat tail and webbed back feet that make them well adapted to a life in water – they are excellent swimmers. They live mainly in holes in the river bank, but in the north they may build dams to create pools in which to build their home, called a lodge. The entrance is always under water. The animals

feed on a variety of plant materials, including the bark of trees and shrubs.

Bedbug

Bedbug A small wingless insect which feeds by sucking blood from humans and animals. Bedbugs come out at night to feed. They give off an unpleasant, oily smell and their bite irritates the skin. Though bedbugs were once common, they are now becoming scarce.

Bedstraw A group of herbs with weak stems supporting whorls of narrow leaves and small, usually white flowers. The name comes from the days when they were used to stuff pillows and mattresses.

Bee A group of insects related to ants and wasps. Some bees, such as the familiar HONEY BEE, are social insects, living in colonies. The queen lays eggs, most of which produce infertile females called workers who tend the nest and new young; others produce males (drones) and new queens. BUMBLE BEES are also social bees, though they are not so highly organized as honey bees and have smaller nests which last for only one summer. Solitary bees, such as the MINING BEE, nest in burrows in the ground. Bees can sting, but are not normally aggressive. They feed on nectar and pollen from flowers, the

Beavers

honey bee using much of the nectar to make honey. A 'language' of body movements is used by bees to tell one another where to find flowers. See also CARPENTER BEE and LEAF-CUTTER BEE.

Beech A large, strong deciduous tree growing up to 30 metres tall. The fruit, known as beechmast, consists of a hairy green husk which dries and splits open to release one or two shiny brown triangular nuts. Some beeches have purple leaves and are called copper beeches. All have smooth grey bark, oval leaves and slender pointed buds.

Bee-fly Although these insects are true flies, most look like bees. They have hairy bodies and long mouth parts with which to suck nectar from flowers. The larvae of some bee-flies live as parasites on solitary bees, beetles or grasshoppers.

Bee-fly

Beefsteak fungus A bracket fungus with flesh the colour and texture of raw beef. It also 'bleeds' when damaged. It grows singly, mainly on the stumps and trunks of oak. The fan-shaped or hoof-like bracket has a yellowish underside.

Beetle One of the most widespread groups of insects, recognized by their hard wing-covers, or elytra, which are modified forewings. They

Beech

protect the delicate hind wings. Beetles look similar to bugs, but have biting jaws rather than sucking mouth parts, as bugs have. Although they can fly, most beetles are ground-dwellers, and many are burrowers. They eat almost anything, including other insects, plants, carrion and dung. Many beetle larvae are pests, damaging plants and trees. Like butterflies, beetles have a four-stage life cycle. From the egg hatches a larva or grub, which grows by shedding its skin. The larva eventually turns into a pupa, from which the adult beetle emerges. There are about 330,000 species of beetle, making up the insect group Coleoptera. The name Coleoptera comes from two Greek words meaning 'sheath-wing'.

Bellflower A family of plants with generally blue, bell-shaped flowers. Most, like the HAREBELL, grow upright with pointed leaves; the creeping ivy-leaved bellflower is an exception.

Betony A small flowering plant that produces reddish-purple flowers, arranged in tight oblong spikes, and has heart-shaped leaves. Betony is often used in herbal medicine.

Biennial A plant that completes its life cycle in two years. In the first year it stores food; the food is used during the second year when the plant flowers and produces seeds. The plant then dies.

Bilberry Short deciduous undershrub of the heath family. It produces a characteristic purple bloom, and an edible black berry often used for making jam. Usually found on moors and heaths, it can also survive at high altitudes.

Bindweed A family of creeping or climbing plants with open trumpet-shaped flowers and heart- or arrow-shaped leaves. There are several species of bindweed. The hedge bindweed is very common and covers hedges with a cloak of huge white flowers. The field bindweed has small pink and white blooms and is a weed of farms and gardens.

Hedge bindweed

Bioluminescence Light given out by living things as a result of special chemical reactions in their bodies. Female glow-worms give out light to attract the males. Male and female fireflies both flash their lights to attract each other. Many deep-sea fishes also glow, either to attract and find food or to attract mates. Virtually no heat is produced with the light.

Birch A group of deciduous trees and shrubs, most of which have triangular leaves. The flowers are arranged in spikes called catkins. The male catkins are usually long and hanging; the female catkins are shorter, and some stand erect. The tiny seeds are scattered by the wind, and birches are among the first trees to spring up on bare ground. The silver birch is one of the most common species. It is a graceful tree that grows up to 30 metres high and produces winged fruit. Its bark, silvery white and peeling, gives the

Bird's-nest fungus

Silver birch

tree its name. Another species, the dwarf birch, grows further north than any other tree or shrub.

Birch bracket　A bracket fungus found on birch trees throughout the year. The brackets are rather hoof-shaped and have a corky texture. The fungus attacks living trunks and often kills them.

Bird　A warm-blooded vertebrate whose forelimbs are highly modified as wings. Its body is covered in feathers and it has a beak and no teeth. Birds reflect some of their reptilian ancestry in that they have scaly legs and feet and lay eggs. Most are well adapted for flight, with large flight muscles attached to a broad breast bone, and light bones, many of which are hollow. There are several species that are flightless, though none of these lives in NW Europe. Birds belong to the class Aves.

Bird's nest fungus　One of a group of fungi that, when ripe, have fruiting bodies that resemble little nests with

eggs in. The spores develop inside the 'eggs'. Raindrops splash out the 'eggs' which then split open to allow the spores to escape.

Bistort　A short unbranched flowering plant, frequently found near water in fields and woods. The amphibious bistort is often found growing in water. Both species have small pink flowers arranged in thick spikes.

Bistort

Bittercress　Several species of white-flowered plant related to the cabbage. The hairy bittercress is a common garden weed with a rosette of hairy leaves at the base of its stem. The large bittercress has a bitter taste. It is found by streams and other damp places.

Bitterlings

Bitterling A freshwater fish belonging to the carp family, found all over central and eastern Europe. It is a small fish, never more than 9 cm long. It lives in weed-filled ponds and slow-running rivers. The female lays her eggs in freshwater mussels. The male then sheds his sperm over the shell to fertilize the eggs. When the larvae hatch they swim away, leaving the mussel unharmed.

Bittern A heron-like bird of reeds and marshes. It has a brown, speckled plumage and when still, with its bill pointed skywards, it is hard to spot among the reeds. Bitterns feed on frogs, fishes and small water animals. The male bird has a deep booming call.

Bittersweet A low-growing, downy plant, related to the deadly nightshade, and found in woods and scrub. Its bright purple flowers are arranged in loose clusters and the plant produces poisonous, red, oval-shaped berries.

Bivalve Member of a group of aquatic · molluscs whose shells consist of two hinged valves. The group includes mussels, clams and oysters.

Black-backed gull Gulls similar in appearance to the herring gull but with darker grey, almost black backs. There are two species: the greater black-backed gull and the lesser (smaller) black-backed gull.

Blackberry See BRAMBLE.

Blackbird A common member of the thrush family. The male is all black with a bright yellow beak; the female is a dull brown with a slightly mottled breast and a dull beak. Blackbirds are fine songsters. When agitated they utter a persistent 'pink, pink' which serves as an alarm call for all the birds around. Blackbirds in the extreme north of Europe migrate in the winter.

Blackcap A warbler whose dark crown – black for the male, dark brown for the female – distinguishes

Blackcaps

male   female

21

it from the similar garden warbler. The bird's song is sometimes mistaken for that of the nightingale. Blackcaps live in woods and heaths and most fly south for the winter.

Blackfly See APHID.

Black-headed gull A seabird common around European coasts. In winter, it looks very like the common gull but in summer it is

Bladderwort Several species of aquatic, insect-eating plant. They have no roots, but grow suspended in still water. Their submerged leaves have small pouches attached to them which trap and digest small water fleas.

Blanketweed A group of filamentous green algae found in fresh or brackish water.

Bleak

distinguished by its brownish-black head. It also has distinctive red legs and bill. Like many other gulls, the black-headed gull ranges inland, feeding in flocks; many now breed inland and never go to sea.

Blackthorn A small deciduous tree or shrub belonging to the rose family and often found in hedges. It is also called sloe. It has black bark, long sharp thorns and small white spring flowers in dense spikes. Its small blackish-purple fruit is used for making jams or wine and sloe gin.

Blackthorn

Bleak A small silvery freshwater fish, generally about 13 cm long, which lives in shoals in slow-flowing streams and clear lakes. It belongs to the carp family and is found over most of central and northern Europe.

Blenny Member of a group of small fishes found around European coasts, usually on rocky shores. All blennies have a fin running nearly the whole length of their back. The group includes the BUTTERFISH and the EEL-POUT.

Blewit A stocky toadstool whose colour ranges from pale tan to grey. The stalk is violet, the gills are white to flesh-coloured and spores are pale pink. The fungus grows in grasslands where it often forms fairy rings. The wood blewit varies from chestnut brown to violet.

Blood-vein moth A European moth, with pink to purple wings, striped across with a single red 'vein'. It is seen around woodland edges and over damp ground. The caterpillar is grey with four dark spots along the back.

Bloodworm The bright red larvae of certain non-biting midges which live in stagnant water.

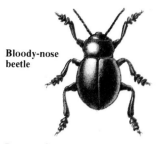

Bloody-nose beetle

Bloody-nose beetle Two species of beetle which, like the blister beetle (which causes blisters on the skin), use a 'chemical' weapon for defence. They spit out a red blood-like liquid which, although not harmful, causes a would-be enemy to halt – giving the beetle more time to escape.

Blow-fly See BLUEBOTTLE.

Blue Name of a widespread group of butterflies. The males are blue, the females often brown with only hints of blue. The large blue is particularly interesting because its caterpillars are collected by ants and taken into the ants' nest. There they are fed on ant larvae, giving off, in exchange, a sweet fluid which is eaten by the ants. The caterpillars spend the winter in the ants' nest, pupate, then fly away as winged adults in the spring.

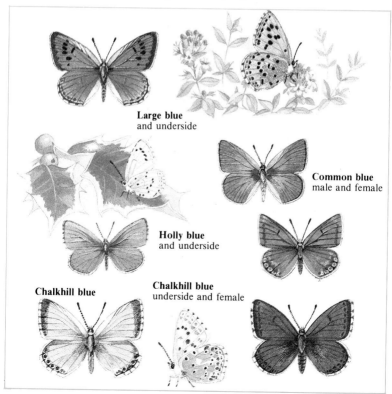

Large blue
and underside

Common blue
male and female

Holly blue
and underside

Chalkhill blue

Chalkhill blue
underside and female

Bluebell Short spring flower belonging to the lily family, which carpets woods, sea cliffs and mountains in spring with its sky-blue, bell-shaped flowers. The long narrow leaves grow directly from the bulb and the flowers are arranged in a long spike. The flowers can also be pink or white. In Scotland, the term bluebell is applied to the harebell and the bluebell is better known as wild hyacinth.

Bluebottle

Bluebottle Several species of large, metallic blue flies, also called blowflies. They have a buzzing flight and are disliked because they spread disease and spoil food. Bluebottles lay their eggs on rotting flesh, meat and fish. The eggs hatch into white larvae or maggots about a day later.

Blue shark A dangerous shark named for its colour. It grows up to 4 metres long and lives in the open oceans, occasionally visiting the North Sea. It is also called the blue whaler.

Bluethroat A bird related to the robin. It nests close to the ground and frequents marshy woodland and heathland. The male has a blue throat. Scandinavian birds have a red spot in the blue patch; birds from further south have a white spot.

Blue tit The commonest tit and the one most adapted to life with people, frequently seen in gardens feeding at bird-tables. It has bright blue markings on its head, wings and tail, a green back and yellow underparts, and a black streak running through the eyes. It has an undulating flight and can climb up tree trunks in search of insects. See picture on page 172.

Blusher A woodland toadstool that gets its name because its white flesh turns pink when cut or bruised. The cap is reddish brown, usually with white flakes of skin, and the gills are white. There is a ring near the top of the stem.

Boar, wild A wild pig once common in Britain and northern Europe but

Wild boar and piglets

now extinct in this area. It is still widely distributed in the forests of southern and central Europe.

Bogbean An aquatic creeping plant commonly found in bogs, marshes and ditches. The leaves and flowers grow above the surface of the water but the stems creep through the mud at the bottom. The pink and white flowers are fringed with white hairs and borne in spikes.

Bolete

Bolete Member of a group of toadstools in which the underside of the cap is sponge-like, with masses of tiny pores instead of gills. The spongy part is easily detached from the rest of the cap. Several species are very good to eat and only the DEVIL'S BOLETUS is poisonous.

Borage A bristly garden plant with cucumber-scented juices and bright blue flowers arranged in leafy clusters. It was once commonly used in medicine and cooking.

Box An evergreen tree with small, leathery leaves. It grows very slowly, reaching a height of 10 metres. The single-sexed greenish flowers have no petals and grow in small clusters at the base of the leaves. The tree grows in many parts of Europe, especially on lime-rich soils.

Box elder See MAPLE.

Brachiopod See LAMPSHELL.

Bracken A common fern that grows in woods, moors and heaths, frequently forming a complete ground cover to the exclusion of all other plants. Bracken has a series of underground stems called rhizomes which spread quickly, throwing up leaves over a large area. It was once of great economic importance as a source of potash (a form of potassium carbonate), used in the production of soap and glass.

Bracket fungus A fungus that grows on trees, with a fruiting body shaped like a shelf or bracket. There are many species, nearly all belonging to the group known as polypores. The lower surface of the bracket bears thousands of tiny pores like those found in the boletes. Bracket fungi usually attack dead trunks and branches, but some attack living trees and may actually kill them.

Bracket fungus

Bract Small leaf growing at the point where a flower-bearing stem joins another stem or branch.

Bramble A thorny, rambling shrub belonging to the rose family. It has white or pink flowers and produces the blackberries that are so commonly collected for making jams and pies. Brambles are found in woods and hedgerows and on open waste ground.

Brambling A bird belonging to the finch family, distinguished in flight by its white rump. The male has an almost black head and back in summer and an orange breast throughout the year. Females and winter males are duller, with brown heads. They breed in northernmost Europe but move south in winter in huge flocks in search of good crops of beech seeds. In their breeding area they feed largely on insects.

Bream A freshwater fish belonging to the carp family, with a deep, flattened body measuring about 35 cm long. It likes slow-moving or even stagnant waters. Some spend part of their time in brackish waters. Bream feed on worms and other animals of the muddy river bottom.

Brambling

Brent goose A winter visitor from Greenland and northern Russia which is usually found close to the sea, feeding on sea-grass and sand worms. Brent geese are smaller than other geese (roughly the same size as a mallard duck). The plumage is grey-brown, with a black head and neck, and white undersides.

Silver bream

Bream

Brill A flatfish closely related to the turbot. It is smaller and slimmer than its cousin, 50 cm long, and does not have any bony platelets. It feeds on bottom-living fishes and crustaceans, and normally lies on its right side.

Brimstone

Brimstone butterfly The male of this species is a bright yellow, while the female is greenish-white. Brimstone butterflies may be found flying in gardens, hedgerows and woodland; they feed on buckthorn. They hibernate in evergreen bushes during the winter, their leaf-like wings giving them good protection.

Brimstone moth A yellow moth with brown spots, usually seen in early

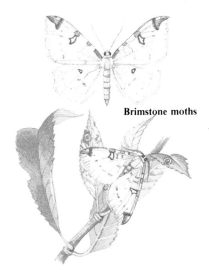

Brimstone moths

summer. The larva or caterpillar is a looper – that is, it moves by raising the middle section of its body into the air and pushing the front end forwards. It has legs only at the front and tail ends, and looks just like a brown twig.

Bristletail A group of primitive wingless insects with either two- or three-pronged tails. They live beneath stones and leaves, and some live in houses. There are some 350 species, including the SILVERFISH which is a three-pronged bristletail.

Bristletails

Bristle worm A group of marine annelid worms that have bundles of bristles on each segment of their bodies. They are commonly found on the seashore and include the lugworms, fanworms and ragworms.

Brittle gill Member of a group of toadstools whose gills break very easily. The toadstools are usually strongly domed at first but they flatten out and often become funnel-shaped. The caps are frequently brightly coloured and the gills are usually white.

Brittle star A group of star-shaped marine creatures belonging to the same phylum as the starfishes – the echinoderms. Brittle stars have five slender, spiny arms that easily break off but regrow quickly. They feed by filtering tiny food particles from the water or by sifting through the debris on the sea bed. Those with many-branched, coiled arms are called basket stars. Brittle stars are also known as sand stars or serpent stars.

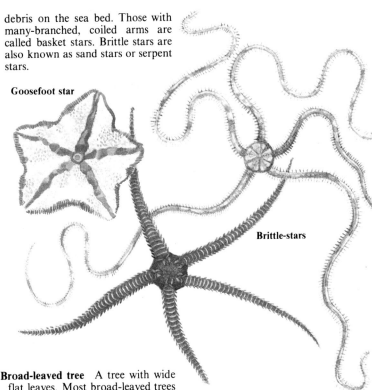

Goosefoot star

Brittle-stars

Broad-leaved tree   A tree with wide flat leaves. Most broad-leaved trees have strong hard timber and are frequently called hardwoods. They are all flowering plants and are Europe's most common trees, though they do not grow in the colder north or in high mountain regions. Most are deciduous but a few, such as the holly and the holm oak, are evergreen.

Brooklime   A widespread, low-growing large speedwell plant which produces blue flowers arranged in stalked spikes. It grows in wet places, particularly in mud.

Broom   Several deciduous gorse-like shrubs, which belong to the pea family. The twigs are ridged and support the golden-yellow flowers. The flowers have a trip mechanism which sprays any insect alighting on them with pollen. Unlike gorse leaves, those of the broom do not form sharp spines. Broom is found covering areas of dry heathland.

Broomrape   A parasitic plant which grows on the roots of other flowering plants. It does not contain the green pigment chlorophyll and has scales instead of leaves. There are many species of this plant, each specific to one or two hosts. The common broomrape is the most familiar species, often found growing on peaflowers. Its flowers are purplish or creamy, arranged in a spike.

Small heath

Meadow brown

Grayling

Ringlet

Great banded grayling and underside

Marbled white

Brown A fairly common family of butterflies, most of which are orange or brown in colour. Examples are the SPECKLED WOOD, RINGLET, GATE-KEEPER and meadow brown butter-flies. The caterpillars of brown butterflies generally feed on grasses.

Brown owl See TAWNY OWL.

Bryophyte Member of a small group of low-growing flowerless plants comprising the liverworts and mosses.

Buck The male of several species of animal including fallow deer, roe deer, reindeer, hare, rabbit, ferret and rat.

Buckthorn A group of shrubs or small trees, with tiny green flowers arranged in clusters. The common buckthorn is a thorny shrub, often used for hedging. It produces clusters of black berries from which comes the dye 'sap-green'.

Bud A tight cluster of leaves surrounding an undeveloped shoot, or an unopened flower.

Budding (1) Process by which some lower invertebrates reproduce asexually. It involves the formation of an outgrowth from the side of an organism which eventually breaks away to form a new individual. Hydra is an organism that reproduces in this way. (2) Method of grafting which involves attaching a bud to another plant in such a way that the two parts will grow together as a single plant.

Buddleia A group of about 70 species of deciduous and evergreen shrubs. The most common species in Europe is a native of China. It is often called the butterfly bush because its magnificent purple flowers attract so many butterflies in summer.

Buff-tip When at rest, with its wings pulled in tight against its body, the buff-tip moth looks just like a dead twig. Its wings are greyish-brown, and it is often found in orchards. The forewings have a buff (sand-coloured) patch at the tip.

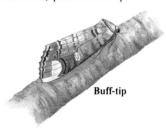

Buff-tip

Buddleia

Red admiral

Peacock

Small tortoiseshell

Bug, true Many insects may be called 'bugs'. But true bugs are insects which look rather like beetles, though with different mouth parts. Bugs feed by piercing and sucking the juices from plants or animals, and their mouth parts form pointed 'beaks'. (Beetles have jaws for

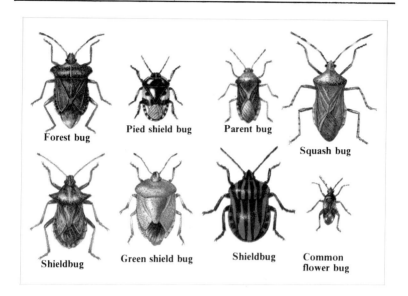

Forest bug

Pied shield bug

Parent bug

Squash bug

Shieldbug

Green shield bug

Shieldbug

Common flower bug

chewing.) Bugs live on and under water as well as on land, and some, such as the aphid and leafhopper, can be pests. Other examples of bugs are the stinkbugs, water boatmen and cicadas.

Bugle A low creeping plant with bright blue flowers arranged in a long leafy spike. It grows in woodlands and spreads by means of runners.

Bugloss Several short hairy plants of the borage family. The viper's bugloss is a common species. Its pink buds and bright blue flowers add a splash of colour to gardens and wastelands. The name bugloss means 'ox-tongued' in Greek, an apt term for the rough, tongue-shaped leaves.

Bulb Underground reproductive organ and food store of certain plants consisting of a short stem surrounded by thick fleshy leaves. New shoots grow from buds formed in the axils of the leaves. After

flowering, a new bud swells up with food to form a new bulb. Tulips and onions are both bulbs. See also CORM.

Bullfinch A beautiful bird, disliked by fruit-growers because it eats the buds of fruit trees. Both sexes have black caps and the male has a bright red breast. Bullfinches live in Europe all the year round and only the most northerly birds migrate south. They are usually seen in pairs and apparently mate for life. They nest in thick bushes or hedges.

Bullfinches

female

male

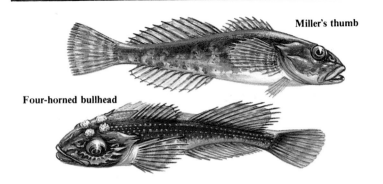

Miller's thumb

Four-horned bullhead

Bullhead Member of a group of mainly freshwater fishes belonging to the sculpin family. The most common species is the miller's thumb. It has a large bulbous head and gets its curious name from the tradition that a miller's thumb was wide through continually rubbing grains between thumb and fore-finger. It is a rather spiny fish, about 10 cm long, and lives in stony, swift-flowing streams.

Bulrush A tall, wind-pollinated plant found in shallow water. Its long stem supports a large brown cylindrical body, consisting of tiny, tightly-packed female flowers. Above this, the paler male flowers form a slender spike. The bulrush is a common freshwater plant, and is also known as the great reedmace or cattail. The lesser bulrush is a smaller and less common relative.

Bumble bee A group of large bees with a slow, droning flight. When visiting flowers to feed, the hairs on the bumble bee's body become dusted with pollen. As the bee passes among the flowers it helps to pollinate them. Bumble bees live in small colonies, usually nesting underground. Only the queens survive the winter and fresh colonies are founded every spring. Most species are black with yellow, red or white markings. One of the largest or these chunky bees is the buff-tailed bumble bee.

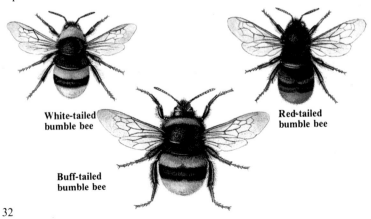

White-tailed
bumble bee

Red-tailed
bumble bee

Buff-tailed
bumble bee

Ortolan buntings

Bunting A family of seed-eating birds that look similar to finches, with stout bills for cracking open seeds and nuts. Buntings tend to be less well known than finches because they are not so colourful and do not frequent parks and gardens. See CIRL BUNTING, CORN BUNTING, REED BUNTING and YELLOWHAMMER.

bodies contain cyanide poison. Burnet moths have antennae with knobs at the ends, and so may be confused with butterflies. The larvae spin yellowish cocoons, often high up on grass stems. After the adult has emerged, the empty pupal skin can often be found hanging from the cocoon. The most common species is the six-spot burnet which has six red spots on each of its shiny black forewings.

Burnished brass A brown moth with metallic yellow markings (sometimes almost green) on the wings. It is a relative of the silver-Y moth, and like it has clumps of hair along the back of its body.

Bur-reed A family of hairless, freshwater plants with long, iris-like leaves. The single-sexed flowers form small, green, globular heads. Some species, such as the branched bur-reed, stand erect at the water's

Burbot

Burbot The only member of the cod family that lives in fresh water. It is a slender fish, about 40 cm long. The barbel on its lower jaw serves as a feeler. Burbot live in lakes and slow-moving rivers, feeding on the bottom at dawn and dusk. They eat fishes and various invertebrates.

Burnet moth A group of black and red day-flying moths. The bright colour is a warning, since the moths'

edge, while others float freely.

Burying beetle A group of carrion beetles (beetles which feed on the bodies of dead animals). They are also known as sexton beetles, named after the people who tend graves in churchyards. The male and female beetles work together when they find a corpse such as that of a mouse, digging out the soil from underneath it so that eventually the body is

Black burying beetle

buried. The burying beetles eat the carrion, and also lay their eggs on it.

Butterbur A short plant related to the daisy, whose leaves may be up to 1 metre across when full-grown. The light clusters of pink flowers appear before the leaves. Male and female flowers grow on separate plants. Butterburs form patches in damp places such as riverbanks, water-meadows and roadsides.

Buttercup Several species of flowering plant characterized by their waxy, yellow, five-petalled flowers. They have poisonous juices and are therefore avoided by grazing animals. The most common species is the meadow buttercup which grows mainly in meadows and other damp, grassy places. It grows up to 1.2 metres tall. The shorter bulbous

Meadow buttercup

buttercup can be identified by its downward-turned sepals. It likes drier ground than the meadow buttercup.

Butterfish A small fish found in shallow coastal waters around northern Europe. It belongs to the blenny family and is also known as the gunnel. The fish grows up to 24 cm long and has 9–13 black spots along its dorsal fin. The female lays her eggs in a large ball, and wraps herself round it to protect them.

Butterfly Among the most beautiful of insects, butterflies are generally more colourful than their close relatives, the moths. Both insects have large wings and feed on flowers. Butterflies can generally be distinguished from moths by the knobs on the ends of their antennae. Moths rarely have these. After mating, the female butterfly lays eggs which hatch into larvae called caterpillars. The caterpillar feeds on plants and eventually turns into a chrysalis or pupa, inside which it changes into the adult insect or imago. Most butterflies have short adult lives, but a few species can live through the winter in a state of hibernation.

Butterfly bush See BUDDLEIA.

Butterwort Insect-eating plants related to the bladderwort. The common butterwort has purple, two-lipped flowers and a rosette of sticky, insect-trapping leaves. It is found on moors and bogland.

Buzzard A large, hawk-like bird of prey with broad wings. It soars high in the sky, preferring wooded and hilly country. Buzzards feed on rabbits, mice and other small animals, and have a distinctive mewing cry.

Byssus A cluster of tough, hair-like threads by which certain aquatic molluscs anchor themselves to rock surfaces.

C

Cabbage Several species of flowering plant with four-petalled flowers that resemble a cross. The wild cabbage is the ancestor of many cultivated vegetables. It has a spike of stalked, yellow flowers and greyish leaves. It is often found on sea cliffs and is also known as sea cabbage.

Cabbage moth A common moth whose larva feeds on cabbages and other low-growing plants, as well as the leaves of trees. The cabbage moth is a mottled dark brown, and flies throughout the summer. The caterpillar may be any shade from black to bright green.

Cabbage white See WHITE.

Caddis fly A group of insects which look similar to moths but whose wings are clothed with hairs instead of tiny scales. They are not true flies. Also called sedge flies, some 5000 species are known. Most are dull brown or black. These insects spend their larval stage in water, often

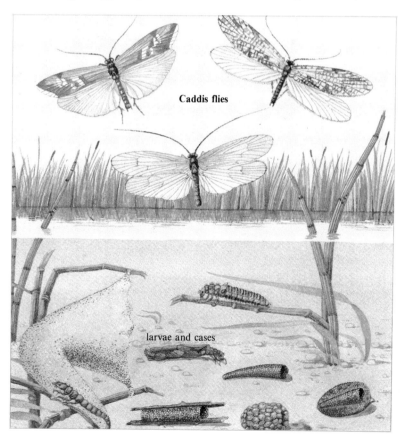

Caddis flies

larvae and cases

building themselves cases of stones, shell fragments and vegetable matter such as leaves. Inside the case, the larva is well hidden and protected from predators.

Calamint Several species of sweet-smelling flowering plant. The common calamint can be recognized by its clusters of purple flowers which bear small dark spots on the petals. It can be found in grassy areas and in woods, those found in woods having considerably larger flowers.

Calf Young (first year) of certain mammals such as domestic cattle and red deer.

Calyx Usually green, outer part of a flower consisting of modified leaves or sepals surrounding the petals. During the bud stage it encloses and protects the rest of the flower.

Camberwell beauty A handsome butterfly with deep brown wings fringed with purple-blue and yellow. Often found in hilly areas, it is particularly fond of ripe fruit and sap oozing from trees. In winter it hibernates. It is named after the London suburb where it was first seen in Britain, but it is only a rare visitor to this country.

Camberwell beauty

Camouflage The means by which various animals avoid detection by would-be enemies by merging with their surroundings. Some animals do this by having a coloration that matches their background. Plaice, for instance, have a colour pattern similar to that of the sea bed on which they live, making them very difficult to detect. They can also change colour to match a change in background colour. Other animals resemble leaves or twigs.

Campion Flowering plants with sepals joined in a tube (inflated in the bladder campion). Red and white campion are common in hedgerows.

Canada goose A large goose introduced from North America as an ornamental bird. It now breeds in the wild in Britain and Scandinavia. The Canada goose is a pale brown in colour, with a black neck and head, save for white patches on the cheeks. Its call is a characteristic 'honk'.

Candle snuff

Candle snuff A small, irregularly shaped fungus consisting of a leathery, strap-like stalk that is very tough and usually forked. Powdery white spores develop near the tips of young stalks, and there are black ones near the base. The fungi can be found at all times of the year on tree stumps and other dead wood.

Candytuft, wild A flowering plant of the cabbage family. It bears clusters of tiny white or purple flowers which are notable for their petals of unequal size. The plant is found in cereal fields and on open ground.

Canopy Top layer of vegetation in a wood or forest, formed by the upper foliage of the trees.

Capercaillie This bird is the largest member of the grouse family. Capercaillies live in northern pine forests, where they feed on pine shoots. The male is black or dark grey and displays before the brown female by fanning out his tail and uttering squawks and screeches.

Capsid bug A large family of insects that are serious pests in many countries. Most have slender or oval brown or green bodies and feed mainly on plants. Some, such as the common green capsid, do great damage to fruit.

Capsid bugs

Carapace The hard cover protecting the head and thorax of certain arthropods such as crabs and prawns. It is made largely of chitin, impregnated with lime for extra hardness. The term also applies to the upper shell of turtles and tortoises.

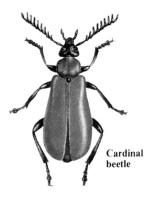

Cardinal beetle

Cardinal beetle Several species of beetle which get their name from their red colour, resembling that of a Roman Catholic cardinal's dress. They live on trees and flowers, and

have feathery antennae. The grubs feed on bark and wood.

Carnivore Any meat-eating animal. More specifically, a term applied to any member of the mammalian order Carnivora which includes the foxes, cats and badgers.

Carp A family of fishes that includes many familiar freshwater species, among them the roach, dace, chub, minnow, carp, and the goldfish so often kept as an aquarium fish. Some species are native to Europe, but others, including the goldfish and the carp itself, have been introduced. Members of this family have no teeth in their jaws, but have teeth in the back of the throat with which they grind up their food. The

Carp

common carp is an Asian fish introduced into Europe by the Romans 2000 years ago. It is a good food fish, often kept in fish farms. In the wild, the carp likes stagnant water or slow-running rivers where it feeds on plants and various small animals. It has barbels on its mouth and, fully-grown, measures more than 20 cm long; a few which reach the age of 40 can be as much as 1 metre long. The crucian carp is a close relative that is smaller than the carp and has no barbels on its mouth. It can flourish in still, muddy waters with little oxygen.

Carpel Female reproductive parts of a flower comprising the STIGMA, STYLE and OVARY. Some flowers, such as the plum, have only one carpel, while others, e.g. the buttercup, have several. After fertilization the carpels form the FRUIT.

Carpenter bee A group of solitary bees, which make their nests in wood. The carpenter bee bores a tunnel up to 20 cm long, lining it with brood cells for its eggs. The cells are made of wood fragments cemented together. Each one is sealed once the egg and a food supply of nectar and pollen have been placed inside.

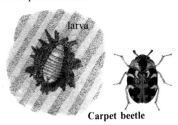
Carpet beetle

Carpet beetle Insects whose larvae feed on rugs, carpets and clothing, including furs. The beetles are about 3 mm long, and look rather like brown ladybirds. They feed on pollen. The larva is very hairy and is known as a woolly bear.

Carpet moth A group of moths which are mottled in colouring, ranging from black to brown, and often difficult to see on tree trunks or

Carpet moths

moss-covered rocks. There are several species, including the common, garden, green and twin-spot carpet moths – all so named because their wings are patterned rather like traditional carpets.

Carpet pin A small fragile toadstool with a thin orange cap and yellowish-brown gills. It grows in damp grassy places in summer and autumn.

Carrion Dead flesh. The carrion-eaters are those creatures which live off already dead animals rather than hunting and catching live prey.

Carrion beetle A family of beetles that eat carrion, the best known being the BURYING BEETLES.

4-spot carrion beetle

Cartilaginous fish Fishes with skeletons of cartilage (gristle) instead of bone, such as sharks, rays and skates. Cartilaginous fishes have no opercula (gill covers) and the gill slits are clearly visible. Their fins are clothed with thick skin, rather than being membranes as in bony fishes.

Catchfly Several species of flowering plant closely related to the campion. Their sepals are fused to form a tube and the flowers are usually either white or pink. The most common is the small-flowered catchfly, a sticky, hairy plant found in dry areas.

Caterpillar Larval stage of certain insects, particularly moths and butterflies. Caterpillars have long soft bodies with three pairs of legs on the thorax and a series of prolegs on the abdomen. They have chewing mouths and are mostly vegetarian. As they grow, caterpillars moult several times before they are ready to pupate (see PUPA).

Catfish A group of about 2000 species of fish, of which only one is native to northern Europe. Catfishes have no scales but all have long barbels on the mouth. The wels or European catfish is a large freshwater fish with a long body and a broad, flat head. Most grow to

Common cat's-ear

Catmint A mint-scented, downy, grey plant with red-spotted white flowers growing in whorls. Found in hedge-banks and among rocks.

Cat's-ear Several species of herb

American catfish

about 1 metre long, but it has been known to reach 5 metres. It feeds mainly on other fishes, but also catches ducklings, frogs and water voles.

Catkin Cluster of single-sexed flowers arranged on a spike and often long and hanging. The term is most commonly applied to the male flowers of trees such as hazels, willows and poplars.

belonging to the daisy family and looking similar to the dandelion. The common cat's-ear has a rosette of hairy leaves at the base of its stem. It produces solitary yellow flower-heads and is found in fields and meadows.

Cauliflower fungus A fungus that forms pale, cauliflower-like masses at the base of conifer trunks in autumn, up to 30 cm across.

Cedar Member of a group of tall coniferous trees belonging to the pine family. The needles are borne in dense whorls and the cones are like upright barrels which fall to pieces when the seeds are ripe. The cedar of Lebanon is a native of the eastern Mediterranean but is widely planted as an ornamental tree. It grows up to 40 metres tall and has a massive trunk with wide, sweeping branches, and a flat-topped crown. Some trees live up to 2000 years. There are three other kinds of true cedar, but the name also applies to certain members of the cypress family. Examples include the white cedar, a North American species grown in Europe for hedging or for ornament, and the western red cedar. The latter, also from North America, is quick-growing (up to 40 metres) and commonly planted for shelter and timber.

Greater celandine

Cedar of
Lebanon

Celandine Two unrelated species of plant, both bearing yellow flowers. The greater celandine is related to the poppy and has an easily broken stem which has bright orange sap. The lesser celandine is related to the buttercup and has shiny heart-shaped leaves. They are both common in hedgebanks.

Cellulose Substance (carbohydrate) found in most plants, forming the main element of cell walls. Its fibrous nature makes it an important raw material in the textile industry in the form of cotton and flax.

Centaury Several species of upright plant, of which only the common and the slender centaury are

Common centaury

widespread. Both bear pink flowers, arranged in tight clusters, usually open only in bright sunlight.

Centipede A group of many-legged arthropods that have between 15 and 177 pairs of legs. Their flat bodies are made up of many segments, with a pair of legs on all but the last two. The first pair of legs form poisonous fangs. Centipedes live in damp places, under stones or in houses, hunting other small invertebrates at night.

Cephalopod Member of a group of marine molluscs containing squids, octopuses and cuttlefish. Cephalopods differ from other molluscs in many respects. They have a distinct head surrounded by arms with suckers on them; and the shell (when present) is internal, enclosed in the mantle (the thick layer of skin common to all the molluscs). The mantle does not cover the head completely; instead it ends in a loose

Garden chafer

Rose chafer

Chafer A group of beetles which live on plants and may be seen in gardens. The best known chafer is the COCKCHAFER or maybug. Another common species is the rose chafer, a sturdy green insect sometimes found on rose flowers. The beetles' larvae feed on wood and roots.

Chaffinch The commonest of the finches, it lives in Europe all the year round, but moves south in winter

Chaffinches

female

male

'collar' around the neck. The cephalopod breathes by drawing water under the collar into the mantle cavity and over the gills. The water is then passed out through a muscular tube called the siphon. By squirting it out at speed the animal creates a form of jet propulsion by which it moves rapidly through the water.

Chaeta Bristle, particularly common on annelid worms.

from northern Scandinavia. The bird is easily identifiable by the two white wing bars on its dark wings. The female is a duller coloured bird than the male, which has a grey-blue crown and an orange-pink breast. The nest is built in an open site in a tree or hedge, but is well camouflaged.

Chamomile A group of generally fragrant herbs that bear small daisy-like flowerheads.

Chanterelle A yellow funnel-shaped toadstool that smells of apricots and grows in deciduous woods. The outer or lower surface bears a maze of irregular folds. The false chanterelle is less fleshy and more orange than the true chanterelle. It grows mainly in coniferous woods.

Charlock Often known as wild mustard, charlock is a tall flowering weed of the cabbage family. It is a hairy plant with bright yellow flowers and is found in arable fields.

Charlock

Charr, Arctic A relative of the trout, commonly found in mountain lakes. Some Arctic charr migrate to the sea after spawning. They grow up to 1 metre long.

Chela Claw or pincer of certain arthropods such as crabs and lobsters.

Cherry, wild A deciduous tree belonging to the rose family and the ancestor of all cultivated sweet cherries. It grows up to 20 metres tall and is sometimes called the gean. Its small sweet fruits are eaten by birds which pass the stones and help to spread the trees. The closely related bird cherry is often found growing alongside streams, especially in more northerly regions. Both trees

Wild cherry

are covered with white flowers in spring.

Cherry plum A deciduous tree belonging to the rose family, also known as the myrobalan. It originated in the Balkans and Asia, and is grown in many parts of Europe for its fruit. It is also used as a hedging plant and grows about 8 metres tall. Its white flowers look similar to blackthorn blossom, and the tree is one of the earliest to flower in spring.

Cherry plum

Chestnut See SWEET CHESTNUT and
HORSE CHESTNUT.
Chickweed Several species of small,
common weed that bear tiny white
flowers. The common chickweed is a
straggling plant with a single line of
hairs running down its stem. It is
found in abundance on cultivated
land.
Chicory A flowering plant related to
the dandelion. It has a stiff, many-
branched stem with bright blue
flowers arranged in a spike. It is
often found in areas of wasteland,
and its leaves can be used for making
salad.

Chicory

Chiffchaff A small warbler that is
easily distinguished from its close
relatives the willow warbler and the
wood warbler by its call, 'chiff-chaff,
chiff-chaff', from which it gets its
name. It has a greyish-green
plumage and lives in woods and
bushy places, building its nest in

brambles or other undergrowth.
The bird is a summer visitor from
Africa and southern Europe.
Chimaera Like their relatives, the
sharks and rays, the chimaeras are
cartilaginous fishes. They are unusual among cartilaginous fishes in
that the gill slits are covered by an
operculum (gill cover). They are also
known as rabbitfishes. The common
rabbitfish lives close to the sea bed,
feeding on crustaceans, molluscs
and echinoderms, plus small fishes.
The female is larger than the male,
up to about 120 cm long.
Chinese water deer A native of
China, now established in wild herds
in England and France. It is a small
deer, about 50 cm high at the
shoulder, and has long upper canine
teeth that project below the upper
lip. Neither males nor females have
antlers. The deer are not often seen
because they feed mostly at night.
Chitin Tough, resistant substance
common to certain invertebrates. It
forms the exoskeleton of insects and
crustaceans and the chaetae
(bristles) of annelid worms.
Chiton A group of primitive marine
molluscs, also called coat-of-mail
shells from the eight hinged plates
that make up their outer coat.
Chitons graze on algae on rocky
shores, attaching themselves to the
rocks like limpets. They can also

Chiffchaffs

43

Chitons

crawl slowly using their long, single 'foot', and can roll up into a ball for protection.

Chlorophyll Green substance or pigment in most plants by which the organism traps the energy in sunlight during PHOTOSYNTHESIS. It therefore plays a vital role in a plant's ability to make food.

Chordate Any member of the large phylum of animals which includes

and at some stage in their lives the chordates all have a number of gill slits. The latter are often present only in the embryo, but amphibian tadpoles have them and fishes keep them all their lives.

Chough A black bird belonging to the crow family. The common chough (a rather rare bird) has a long, curved red bill and red legs, and lives mainly on sea cliffs. The alpine chough has a shorter yellowish bill and lives high up in mountains.

Chrysalis Pupa or resting stage of butterflies, moths and some other insects.

Chub A freshwater fish belonging to the carp family, found mostly in rivers with clean, gravelly bottoms. It spends the spring and summer in shallow parts of rivers, but migrates to deeper waters, even to lakes, in the winter months.

Chub

all the backboned creatures and a few smaller groups such as the tunicates or sea squirts. In their early stages these animals all have a flexible skeletal rod called the notochord, and it is this that gives the group its name. But the notochord is rapidly replaced by the backbone in most species – even before birth. There is also a hollow nerve cord running along the back,

Cicada Bugs commonly found in warm countries, which 'sing' by vibrating small membranes called tymbals. Usually it is the male cicada which sings. The cicada sucks sap from trees. Only one species is found in Britain, in the New Forest. Some species have a long life cycle, the young remaining as larvae underground for up to 17 years before emerging as adult insects.

Cilium Tiny hair-like structure, usually one of many, on the surface of certain protozoans such as paramecium. The wave-like motion of the cilia creates currents of fluid across the organism, helping it to move and feed. Cilia are also present internally in most other animals, lining passages to help the flow of liquids.

Cinnabar moth A brightly patterned moth, with striking black and red markings which warn birds that it is unpleasant to eat. It flies, not very strongly, over grassy places and is often found near sea coasts. Its caterpillar also displays warning coloration – it is striped yellow and black. The caterpillars are commonly found on ragwort in July and August.

Cinquefoil Several species of mostly creeping plant, of the rose family, with yellow or white flowers. The creeping cinquefoil is a common weed with yellow flowers and long stems that creep along bare ground. Another yellow-flowered member of the group, the spring cinquefoil, is mat-forming and is commonly found in dry grasslands. TORMENTIL is also a cinquefoil.

Cirl bunting A bird of southern Europe whose breeding area reaches as far north as the south of England. It is a duller yellow than the yellowhammer, with which it is sometimes confused, though the male is readily distinguished by its black throat. It lives in scattered trees and bushes.

Clam A bivalve mollusc. Over 12,000 species are known, in both sea and fresh water. Most lie buried in the mud of shallow water, burrowing with their powerful 'foot'.

Clary Several species of flowering

Wild clary

plant, related to the dead-nettle, with fragrant leaves and blue flowers arranged in whorls around a tall spike. The wild clary has purplish stems and white spots on its flowers. It grows on dry grassy areas, particularly on chalk.

Classification The division of all living things into various groups according to how closely the organisms within each group are

male

female

Cirl buntings

related to each other. The first major division is into the two kingdoms: animals and plants. The animal kingdom is further divided into phyla (singular: phylum). There are about 25 invertebrate phyla (containing animals without backbones), but all the vertebrates (animals with backbones) belong to a single phylum, the Chordata. This phylum also includes the tunicates and lancelets (animals with a spinal chord but no backbone). The vertebrates form the sub-phylum Vertebrata. Phyla are divided into classes, e.g. mammals all belong to the class Mammalia. Classes are divided into orders, e.g. the flesh-eating mammals belong to the order Carnivora; orders are divided into families, e.g. all cats belong to the family Felidae; and families are divided into genera (singular: genus). Animals within a genus are usually similar in appearance. The smallest division is the species; each different kind of animal is a separate species.

Plants are not divided into phyla as are animals but into divisions and sub-divisions. After this, the classification of the two kingdoms follows the same pattern of class, order, family, genus, species.

Many species of plant and animal do not have common names. For example, there are over a million species of insect and it would be difficult to give each one a popular name, particularly when some are so similar. Instead, each organism is given a Latin name that can be used throughout the world to identify it. This name consists of the name of the organism's genus followed by its specific name. For instance, the European wild cat is *Felis* (genus) *silvestris* (species). The closely related domestic cat, which belongs to the same genus, is *Felis catus*. The full classification of the wild cat is:

Kingdom:	Animal
Phylum:	Chordata
Class:	Mammalia
Order:	Carnivora
Family:	Felidae
Genus:	*Felis*
Species:	*silvestris*

Cleavers Several species of plants closely related to the bedstraws, and otherwise known as goosegrass. The common cleavers bear tiny hooks that frequently cling to clothing or animal fur. Its flowers are a dull white and the plant is often found straggling over vegetation on waste ground and in hedgerows.

Cleg-fly

Cleg-fly Dull greyish insects related to the horse-fly. Clegs feed by sucking blood from animals. They fly silently and stab their victim before it is aware of their presence.

Click beetle A family of slender beetles named for their habit of righting themselves from an upside-down position with a loud 'click'. The larvae of many click beetles are the garden pests known as wire-worms.

Click beetles

Clouded yellow

Clouded yellow A butterfly which lives on grassy uplands and in open country. Its colour is deep yellow, with dark brown markings. It is a summer visitor to Britain from central and southern Europe.

Clover A large group of small flowering herbs belonging to the pea family. Clovers produce dense rounded flowerheads and have trefoil leaves (leaves made up of three leaflets). They usually form patches in grassy areas. Two of the most common species are the red and white clover, often planted for cattle to eat. Clovers are popular with bees and make tasty honey.

Clubmoss A small group of flowerless green plants that look similar to mosses though they are more closely related to the ferns. Like the ferns, clubmosses have two distinct forms during their life cycle. The dominant form is the spore-bearer; the sexual phase, called the prothallus, is small and normally lives underground – it is therefore rarely seen. The stems of clubmosses are slender with spirally arranged leaves on them. Some plants are mat-forming, others are like small fir trees.

Coalfish See SAITHE.

Coal tit The smallest European tit, easily distinguished from the other black-headed tits (marsh and willow tits) by the white nape of its neck. It is a woodland bird and a frequent garden visitor in winter. It tends to feed on the ground, hunting for seeds and insects. See picture on page 173.

Coat-of-mail shell See CHITON.

Cob A male swan.

Cockchafer Two species of large beetle, also known as maybugs, which fly noisily around gardens in summer. They frequently collide with lighted windows and outside lamps on summer evenings. Their large size (up to 3 cm long) and their orange-coloured feather antennae make them easily recognizable. The cockchafer larva is a white grub which can be a pest, damaging the roots of cereals and other crops.

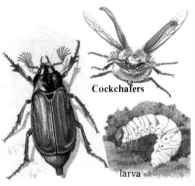

Cockchafers

larva

Cockle Several species of bivalve mollusc with heart-shaped and often ribbed shells. Cockles have a long 'foot' with which to burrow into sand or mud on the sea bed. They can also make short leaps with their 'foot'.

Cockroach A group of beetle-like insects, related to the mantises. They are some of the most widespread and hard-to-destroy pests. Most species live in hot countries, but a few are found in NW Europe. Cockroaches like warmth, and often live in hotels, restaurant kitchens and in the central heating systems of buildings. The common cockroach is dark, with short wings; the German cockroach is paler. The

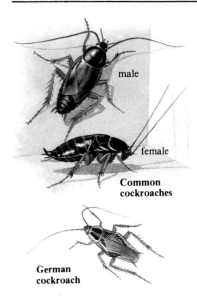

**Common
cockroaches**

**German
cockroach**

smaller dusky cockroach lives outdoors, mostly in trees. All cockroaches have long antennae and long, spiky legs.

Cocoon Silken case spun by many caterpillars as protection when they pupate. Also a similar structure made by other invertebrates, such as earthworms and spiders, to protect their eggs.

Cod One of the most important groups of fishes in Europe is the cod group. Nearly 20 species of the cod family are found in the waters of the North Sea, the Baltic Sea, and the Atlantic Ocean immediately west and north of the British Isles. Also belonging to the group are the lings, hake and rocklings. Most members of the group are large with a distinct lateral line and most have three fins along the back. Many have a barbel on the chin, which helps them to search for food. Most species are bottom-living and do not form shoals. The cod itself is found in colonies across the Atlantic from Newfoundland to the Barents Sea. It grows up to 1.5 metres long.

Coelenterate Member of a group of aquatic invertebrates which includes jellyfishes, hydra, corals and sea anemones. Coelenterates have mostly rounded bodies and display RADIAL SYMMETRY. Their body wall consists of two layers of cells separated by a jelly-like material. They have a central cavity called a coelenteron where they digest their food, and an opening or mouth surrounded by tentacles. The tentacles bear stinging cells which the animals use to stun their prey.

Many coelenterates have two distinct forms during their life cycle – a tubular polyp (like a hydra) and a disc-shaped medusa (like a jellyfish). The two forms alternate with each other in a process known as alternation of generations. The polyps reproduce asexually by budding to produce medusae. These in turn produce sex-cells which fuse to form the polyps. In some

Cod

Whiting

Saithe

Hake

Ling

Haddock

Rockling

coelenterates, such as jellyfishes, the medusa is the dominant form, with the polyp stage insignificant or absent. In other instances, such as with corals and sea anemones, the polyp stage is dominant. Some coelenterates, such as sea anemones, are solitary animals while others, such as corals, form colonies.

Cold-blooded An animal whose body temperature varies with the temperature of its environment is said to be cold-blooded. The animal tends to be slow and lacking in energy when its environment is cold,

and active when it is warmer. The temperature therefore has a major influence on the type of lifestyle the animal can lead. Fishes, amphibians and reptiles are cold-blooded, as are all invertebrates.

Coley See SAITHE.

Collared dove An Asian bird almost unknown in Europe until 1930. Now it lives in most of Europe, where its call, 'coo-cooo-coo', is heard all the year round. It has a distinctive black strap across the back of the neck and nests in conifer trees, mainly near human habitation.

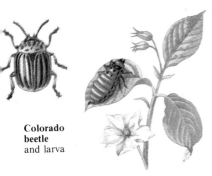

Colorado beetle and larva

Colorado beetle An insect pest which can destroy potato crops. The beetle is about 10 mm long and striped black and yellow. It is native to North America but has spread to Europe where it does great damage. Drastic measures are taken to contain its numbers, particularly in Britain where it has not yet become properly established.

Coltsfoot

Coltsfoot A short creeping plant, with a scaly stem and bright yellow composite flowerheads. Its heart-shaped leaves grow from the roots only after the plant has flowered. Coltsfoot has been used since Roman times as a cough remedy. It is found on bare open ground.

Columbine A tall flowering plant related to the buttercup. It is a woodland plant with attractive hooded flowers which hang down from the branched stem. The petals are usually violet, though occasionally white or pink, and the similarly coloured sepals form long spurs.

Comfrey Several species of hairy flowering plant related to the forget-me-not. The bell-shaped flowers of the common comfrey are either creamy white, pink or purple, and are arranged in clusters. The leaves are long and rough to touch. The common comfrey was formerly used to treat wounds. It is found in very wet areas.

Comma A woodland and garden butterfly which has a comma-like

Comma

mark on its brown underside; the upper side is russet and black. Both sets of wings have noticeably ragged edges. The caterpillar of the comma is disguised to look like a bird-dropping; it feeds on nettles, hops and tree leaves, including elm.

Community Group of plants and animals living together within a given environment.

Composite flower Flower made up of many tiny flowers called FLORETS, each with its own reproductive parts – carpels and anthers. Dandelions and daisies both have composite flowers.

Compound eye Eye of certain invertebrates, particularly insects, made up of thousands of tiny lenses called facets, each of which forms an image. The animal sees an object as a series of tiny images.

Compound leaf A leaf made up of several leaflets arising from a single point, such as the leaves of the horse chestnut.

Cone Reproductive organ of the conifers and related trees (i.e. the gymnosperms). Cones are usually single-sexed, the male, pollen-bearing ones being small and inconspicuous. In most cases, after fertilization, the female cones

spend part of its life in fresh water. It is a greedy predator, feeding on larger sea creatures such as herrings, lobsters and cuttlefishes.

Conifer Member of a group of trees which bear their seeds in cones. Conifers are gymnosperms, and they include such trees as pines, firs, and cedars. Their leaves are generally long and very narrow and for this reason are known as needles. The trees are found throughout NW Europe, particularly in the colder northern parts and mountainous regions where they are able to

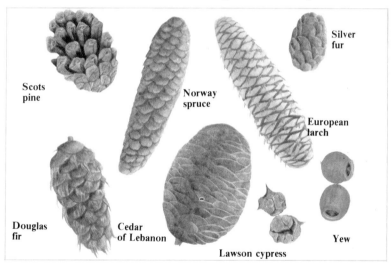

Scots pine

Norway spruce

Silver fir

European larch

Douglas fir

Cedar of Lebanon

Lawson cypress

Yew

become woody. They consist of a series of overlapping scales at the bases of which lie the seeds. In a few cases though, such as the yew and juniper, the mature female cones resemble berries.

Conger eel A long slim fish, closely related to the common eel. Males grow up to 1 metre long, females up to 2 metres. The conger eel lives in rocky coastal waters around Europe and, unlike its cousin, does not

withstand colder climates and higher altitudes than the broad-leaved trees.

Conker Fruit of the HORSE CHESTNUT.

Coot A water bird related to the rails. A plump, short-legged, black bird, the coot has flaps of skin on its toes which help it to swim by paddling. It has a white bill and a white patch on its forehead, and feeds on water animals and plants.

Copepod Member of a large group

Corals

of tiny crustaceans, many of which make up an important part of marine plankton, providing food for fish. Others live in fresh water or damp, mossy places on land. Some species are parasites. Swimming copepods have six pairs of legs arranged down their bodies like oars on a boat. They have large heads and forked tail-ends.

Copper Butterflies with copper-coloured wings marked with darker spots. The large copper is an insect of marshland, while other coppers prefer hilly country. The caterpillars of copper butterflies feed on the leaves of dock and related plants.

Small copper and underside

Coral A large group of sea creatures that live either singly or in colonies. Corals are coelenterates, closely related to the sea anemones, and their bodies are polyps, encased in chalky cups or skeletons. The base of the polyp is attached to a solid surface and around the mouth is a ring of tentacles used for catching food. Only a few species of coral are found around the coasts of NW Europe, and the reef-forming varieties are found only in tropical waters.

Coral spot A fungus whose threads grow through twigs and produce two different kinds of spore-bearing cushions on the surface. The commonest of these are the little pink or orange spots which give the fungus its name. The other kind of cushion is dark red.

Coral spot

Corbie See CROW.

Corm Underground food store of certain plants, e.g. crocus, consisting of a short swollen stem. The corm bears buds and is capable of vegetative reproduction. After a plant has flowered a new corm swells up on top of the old one and new buds form. Corms differ from BULBS in that a stem rather than leaves carries the food store.

Cormorant A sea bird also seen far up rivers. It is black, with short legs and a rather snake-like head. The bill is hooked for catching fish. Cormorants catch their prey by diving, and on land can be seen with wings outstretched when resting.

Corn bunting The largest of the buntings, sometimes called the common bunting. It does not breed in Scandinavia and is rare in the western parts of the British Isles. It has no distinguishing features, being brown with darker streaks, but it can be told apart from similar-looking sparrows by its large size. Corn buntings live in open places such as fields, and in winter the birds gather in large flocks.

Corncrake See RAIL.

Cornflower A pretty, blue-flowering plant related to the daisy and dandelion. It was once very common in cornfields but due to modern farming methods, it is now only found in waste ground.

Corolla Usually brightly coloured part of a flower comprising the petals.

Cotton grass Several species of sedge, commonly found on wet moorland. The flowers are bristly and, after flowering, produce a white cottony material that helps to disperse the seeds.

Cotyledon Leaf inside a seed which, in many cases, grows to form part of the young plant. In some seeds, e.g. beans, the cotyledons act as a food store. Flowering plants are grouped according to whether their seeds contain one cotyledon (the mono-cotyledons) or two (dicotyledons). In gymnosperms the number varies.

Cowberry A flowering shrub of the heath family. It is a low creeping evergreen with clusters of pink or white flowers and tough leaves. It produces edible red berries and is found in woods and on heaths.

Cow parsley A tall, slightly hairy flowering plant of the carrot family. Its small white flowers are arranged in umbrella-like clusters. The hollow ridged stems are often reddish in colour. It is a common plant, often found in hedgerows.

Cowrie Several species of sea snail with thick, egg-shaped shells. The shells are often glossy and speckled. Young cowries have spiral shells which change as they grow until the last whorl covers and hides all the others, leaving only a narrow slit for the opening.

Cowslip A hairy plant related to the primrose that grows in grassy areas. Its short stem supports clusters of deep yellow flowers that bear an orange spot at the base of each petal.

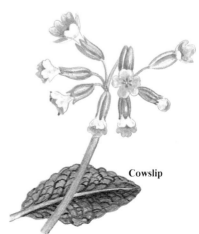

Cowslip

Common cow-wheat

Cow-wheat Several species of small, thin, flowering plant. The common cow-wheat bears pale yellow two-lipped flowers which are arranged in pairs. It is semi-parasitic and is often found in woods attached to the roots of other flowering plants, from which it draws water and minerals.

Coypu A large South American rodent that grows up to 60 cm long. Coypus were once bred in Europe for their fur (nutria) but many escaped and set up colonies, particularly in eastern England, Holland and Germany. They have large heads, webbed feet and a long hairless tail. They live in river banks, doing considerable damage by burrowing, and are expert swimmers.

Crab Crustaceans with five pairs of jointed legs and a broad, flat cover or carapace protecting the body. The abdomen and tail are small and are kept tucked up underneath the trunk. The eyes are on movable stalks and the first pair of legs usually end in grasping claws which the crab uses to catch prey. Most crabs live in the sea but a few are found in fresh water and some on land. One type of crab that does not have a protective cover is the HERMIT CRAB. Instead it lives inside the empty shell of other sea animals, especially whelks.

Crab apple A deciduous tree belonging to the rose family and the ancestor of our eating apples. It grows to a height of 10 metres. Its fruit is too bitter to eat but makes good jelly.

Crake A group of water birds related to the rails and coots. They have mainly streaky brown plumage,

Coypu

and short tails. They seldom fly, preferring to skulk among the reeds of marshes and ponds. The spotted crake is one of the most widespread species though it is not commonly found in Britain. The corncrake is rather rare and, unlike the others, prefers to live on dry ground.

Cranberry A low, creeping, evergreen shrub, bearing edible red berries used for making jelly. Its pink flowers have backward-pointed petals and prominent stamens. The plant grows on marshy ground.

Crane A long-legged bird, rather like a stork but with a shorter bill. Cranes are found in most parts of the world, but most species are rare. They breed in marshy regions, and migrate in flocks, often flying for long distances.

Crane-fly A family of several hundred species of large mosquito-like insect, also known as daddy-long-legs. They have thin bodies with spindly legs and fly rather clumsily. Crane-flies live in gardens and near water. The larvae of many species are known as leatherjackets. They live in the soil and can cause serious damage to crops.

Spotted crane-fly

Shining cranesbill

Cranesbill A group of flowering plants related to the garden geranium, with mainly pink, five-petalled flowers. The name comes from their characteristic fruit which is shaped like a crane's beak.

Crayfish A lobster-like decapod which lives in fresh water, feeding on insect larvae, snails and tadpoles.

Creeping Jenny A low creeping plant related to the primrose. It has yellow, bell-shaped flowers and grows in damp woods.

Crested newt

Crested newt Also called the warty newt because of its coarse black skin. It is up to 14 cm long including the tail, and the male has a ragged crest running down its back in the breeding season. It spends much of its time in water and emits a strong smell when disturbed.

Cricket A group of insects similar to grasshoppers but with much longer antennae. Male crickets sing to the

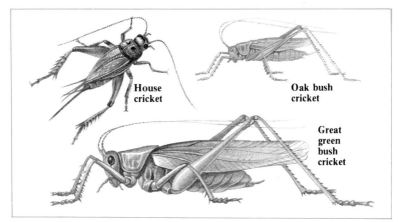

House
cricket

Oak bush
cricket

Great
green
bush
cricket

females by rubbing together their wing-cases. There are two main groups of cricket: the true crickets, which live mainly on the ground and include the field cricket and house cricket; and the bush crickets which live in bushes and other undergrowth. Bush crickets include the great green bush cricket, wart-biter and speckled bush cricket.

Crocus Small flowering plants of the iris family, growing from a corm. The wild spring and autumn crocus have solitary flowers like those of the garden crocuses: six-petalled, purple or white (or both), with orange styles. The flowers of the spring crocus appear between March and April, while those of the autumn crocus come out in September to October, after the long, slim leaves have died.

Crossbill A bird belonging to the finch family. The male is predominantly red, the female yellowish-brown. The crossbill gets its name from its unusual beak, the lower part of which crosses to the

juvenile

Crossbills

male

female

left of the upper part. With this beak the bird can extract seeds from the fir cones on which it feeds. The bird is found in scattered areas of the British Isles. The similar parrot crossbill lives in Scandinavia.

Hooded crow

Crow A family of mainly black birds which includes the rook, jackdaw, jay and magpie. Crows are the largest of the perching birds. They are active and aggressive, with harsh, noisy voices. They eat almost anything, including grain and vast quantities of caterpillars and other insects. Rooks and jackdaws tend to flock together and build their nests in colonies, usually in tree-tops. The carrion crow is completely black with a black beak. It is known as the corbie in Scotland. Carrion crows

crow is a northern form of the carrion crow, but behaves in just the same way.

Crumble cap A fragile toadstool, often found in thousands on rotten logs and tree stumps. The pale yellow cap is bell-shaped and grooved; the gills are grey or black.

Crustacean Member of a group of largely aquatic arthropods which includes crabs, shrimps, barnacles, water-fleas and woodlice. The body is segmented and often divided into three – head, thorax and abdomen. There are several pairs of limbs (the number varying from species to species), commonly branched into two at the end. The head bears two pairs of antennae, the front pair being called antennules. Their function is mainly sensory. Most crustaceans also have compound eyes. The hard exoskeleton is made of chitin, frequently strengthened with deposits of chalk. In several species, e.g. crabs, it forms a large plate or carapace over the front end of the body.

Cub Young of certain mammals, e.g. fox, bear and badger.

Cuckoo A long-tailed, grey bird, about the same size as a kestrel,

Cuckoo

are found almost anywhere. They gather in large flocks in the autumn but, for the rest of the time, they are solitary birds. They have a bad name because they rob nests and eat carrion. The grey-backed hooded

that is often heard and seldom seen. The familiar 'cuckoo' call of the male heralds the spring. Both sexes have a grey head and chest, and grey bars on their pale underparts. They winter in southern Africa and spend April to August in Europe. The female lays her eggs in the nests of other birds, one egg in each nest, removing one of the existing eggs as she does so. When hatched the young cuckoo quickly gets rid of any other chicks or eggs. The foster parents, often much smaller than the cuckoo, have to work very hard for three weeks to satisfy the alien chick's enormous appetite. The young birds follow their parents south in September.

Cuckoo flower Also called lady's smock, the cuckoo flower is a delicate plant belonging to the cabbage family. Its lilac or white flowers appear in the spring, at the same time as the arrival of the cuckoo. The leaves arising from the roots are much finer than those growing from the stem. The plant grows in damp areas, particularly meadows.

Cuckoo-pint See LORDS AND LADIES.

Cuckoo-spit Foam produced by froghopper nymphs to protect themselves from drying up while they feed on plant juices.

Cuckoo wasp A group of parasitic wasps that lay their eggs in the nests of other wasps and bees. The RUBY-TAILED WASP is a common species.

Cup fungus A fungus whose fruiting body is a shallow cup-shaped disc, often brightly coloured, with the spore-producing cells scattered over the upper surface. Most species are small and all are rather brittle. The majority live on the ground, although some grow on dead wood.

Curlew A wading bird of moors and marshes. It uses its long downward-curving bill to dig for insects and small sea cratures on the shore. Some species of curlew fly south in winter, often covering immense distances.

Currant Small deciduous shrubs commonly cultivated for their edible berries. The red and black currant have greenish, five-petalled flowers arranged in drooping spikes, and palmate, lobed leaves. They grow in damp woods and by fresh water.

Cuticle Protective outer covering of most plants and invertebrates. In plants it is made of the substance cutin and its main function is to prevent excessive water loss. In the invertebrates it is either made largely of protein or, as in the case of arthropods, a substance called chitin. The cuticle forms the tough exoskeleton of insects and in crustaceans it is frequently strengthened by deposits of chalk.

Cuttlefish A group of cephalopod molluscs related to the squids, with a chalky inner shell or 'cuttle-bone'. Cuttlefish have streamlined bodies, up to 1.5 metres long. At the head end are eight arms and two long tentacles, all bearing suckers and used to seize prey. Cuttlefish can change colour to camouflage themselves when danger threatens.

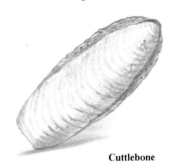

Cuttlebone

Cyclamen A flowering woodland plant related to the primrose. Its heart-shaped leaves, borne on long stems, have a purple tinge on the underside, and the pink or white flowers have backward-turned petals.

Cyclops   A freshwater crustacean. The female is easily recognized by the pair of trailing egg-sacs on either side of the clearly segmented body.

Cyclostome   The most primitive kind of fishes. Cyclostomes have no jaws, only a circular sucking mouth with which they attach themselves to their prey. Their skeletons are made of cartilage (gristle) instead of bone. They include LAMPREYS and HAG-FISHES.

Cygnet   A young swan.

Cypress   A group of coniferous trees found in the cooler northern and southern parts of the world, and on mountains in warmer regions. Cypresses belong to the same family as the junipers. Most species have overlapping scale-like leaves, though young leaves may be needle-shaped. The cones are small and woody. One of the most popular species is the Lawson cypress from the mountains of Oregon and California. It has a conical shape reaching about 35 metres, and is commonly grown in Europe for ornament or shelter.

D

Dab   A flatfish similar to the plaice, but slightly smaller (up to 38 cm long) and found in shallower water. It lives on the sandy sea bed and is particularly common in the North Sea.

Dabchick   See GREBE.

Dace   A freshwater fish belonging to the carp family. It is like a slimmer version of its relative the roach, although it does not have red fins. It can move very quickly and lives in shoals in cool streams and lakes, eating mostly insects.

Daddy-long-legs   (1) See CRANE-FLY. (2) See HARVESTMAN.

Daisy   Several species of flowering plant related to thistles and dandelions. The flowerheads are made up of two types of FLORETS – 'ray' florets surrounding yellow 'disc' florets. The common daisy is a small species found growing in short grass. The leafless stems support solitary flowerheads with white often red-tipped ray florets around the disc

Lawson
cypress

Leyland
cypress

Daisy

florets. The leaves form a rosette at the base of the stem. The ox-eye daisy and the Michaelmas daisy are both taller plants, the latter being well branched.

Damselfly A group of insects related to the dragonflies. Adult damselflies hunt over or near water for small flies such as mosquitoes. They are weak fliers. At rest, they usually fold their wings together, whereas dragonflies keep their wings spread out. Like their relatives, young damselflies live as nymphs in the water, emerging only for their last great change into adults.

Dandelion A widespread flowering plant related to the daisy. Its leafless stems support solitary, bright yellow flowerheads made up of 'ray' FLORETS. The long jagged leaves form a rosette at the base of the stem. The fruits are topped by feathery white 'parachutes' which form the familiar dandelion clock. Dandelion stems contain a milky white juice that was once used in medicine. The leaves may be used in salads and the flowers are used for wine. The name dandelion is a corruption of 'dent de lion', meaning lion's tooth, and referring to the jagged leaves.

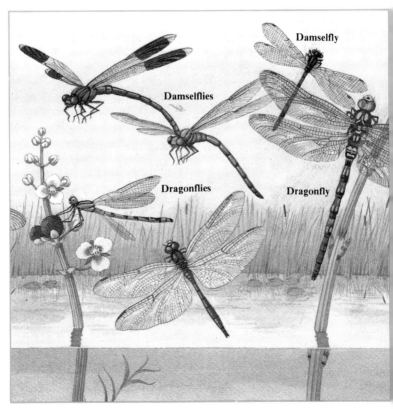

Damselfly

Damselflies

Dragonflies

Dragonfly

Daphnia See WATER FLEA.

Dartford warbler A shy bird, first identified at Dartford, near London, in 1773. It has dark plumage with pinkish-brown underparts, and a long tail. Unlike most other warblers it does not migrate south for the winter. It lives in thick scrub such as gorse and heather.

Darwinism The theory of EVOLUTION by NATURAL SELECTION, as laid out by Charles Darwin in his book 'The Origin of Species', 1859.

Daubenton's bat A small bat, about 4.5 cm long, found in most parts of Europe except the extreme north. It

Daubenton's bat

lives near water and spends most of the night on the wing hunting insects. It often forms large colonies.

Dead-nettle Several species of usually fragrant, flowering plants, whose leaves resemble those of the stinging nettle, though they do not sting. The stem is square and the flowers are two-lipped, arranged in whorls at the base of the leaves. The two most common species are the white dead-nettle, found by the wayside, and the red dead-nettle, an abundant weed of cultivated areas.

Death cap A deadly poisonous toadstool that is fairly common in deciduous woodlands. It has a greenish cap, white gills, a white ring on the stalk, and a ragged bag surrounding the base. The harmless

false death cap has a much yellower cap, often with patches of white skin on it. There is no bag at the base, but the stalk is swollen like a bulb.

Death's head moth See HAWK MOTH.

Deathwatch beetle A wood-boring beetle, renowned for the damage it causes to timber. It gets its name from the sound the adult beetle makes by tapping its head against the walls of its tunnel; this sound was once believed to foretell a death. The larva of the deathwatch beetle feeds on old timber, especially oak. Old buildings, such as churches, are most at risk from deathwatch beetles.

Deathwatch beetle

Decapod (1) Member of a group of crustaceans characterized by having five pairs of walking legs. The group contains the crabs, prawns and lobsters. (2) Member of a group of cephalopod molluscs that have ten arms or tentacles. The group contains the squids and cuttlefishes.

Deceiver, the A toadstool that is common to all kinds of woods and heaths. It gets its name because it occurs in so many forms. The cap is a rich red brown when moist and the stalk is often twisted. The gills are flesh-coloured and widely spaced.

Deer A group of ungulates (hoofed mammals) which are among Europe's largest wild animals. Like cows, deer graze and chew the cud, and usually live in herds. The males

Sika deer

doe

buck

Fallow deer

doe

buck

Roe deer

buck

doe

of most species have antlers which are shed and regrown every year. Each new set of antlers is larger and more branched than those of the previous year. While still growing, antlers are covered with velvet, a smooth covering of skin and short hairs. After growth has stopped, the velvet dries up and the stags can frequently be seen rubbing it off against trees. See CHINESE WATER DEER, ELK, FALLOW DEER, MUNTJAC, RED DEER, REINDEER and ROE DEER.

Desmid A group of single-celled, free-floating algae, often found on the surface of ponds forming a green film.

Devil's boletus Large poisonous toadstool that grows in beechwoods. It can be recognized by its pale cap, blood-red pores, and the red network on the greatly swollen stalk. The flesh is yellow, turning slightly blue in upper regions when damaged.

Devil's coach horse A large black

Devil's coach-horse

rove beetle that adopts a threatening pose, raising its rear end, when disturbed. It also gives off a poison from a gland in its tail. The devil's coach horse is carnivorous, feeding on slugs, snails, and other insects.

Diatom A group of single-celled or colonial algae found in both fresh and salt water. Diatoms have a hard silicon coating that can often look beautiful under a microscope.

Digger wasp Solitary wasps that dig holes in the ground or in dead wood, in which they make their nests. The female drags the paralysed body of a caterpillar or other insect into the nest before laying her egg, so

Digger wasp

providing the wasp larva with food when it hatches.

Dipper A bird of streams and rivers, also called the water-ouzel. It has dark brown feathers, with a white breast, and hops in a characteristic bobbing fashion about the pebbles in a stream, catching insects and other small creatures under the water. The name comes from its constant dipping movement.

Diver Water birds similar to the grebes, and also known as loons.

Divers are excellent swimmers, with short tails, and pointed bills to catch fish. They can stay under water for minutes at a time, but on land can only waddle clumsily. Examples are the great northern and red-throated divers, both of northern regions.

Dock A group of flowering plants with broad, flat leaves and small green flowers arranged in whorls. Often the flowers turn red as they develop into fruits. In the north of Britain docks are frequently called dockens.

Dodder Several species of parasitic leafless climbing plants related to the bindweed. The common dodder has a red stem, and bears fragrant pink flowers. It grows mostly on heather and gorse.

Doe Female of fallow and roe deer, hare or rabbit.

Dogfish Any of several species of small shark. The lesser spotted dogfish is the most common. It is often found on sand banks where it hunts small fishes, molluscs and crustaceans, mostly at night. It grows up to 1 metre long and is covered in brown spots. Also known as the rock salmon or rough hound.

Dog's mercury A poisonous plant with petalless green flowers. The flowers are single-sexed and are borne on separate plants, the males in slender spikes and the females in small clusters. The leaves grow in opposite pairs along the unbranched stem. Dog's mercury often carpets woodlands in the spring.

Dogwood A small deciduous tree or shrub of hedgerows and thickets, especially common on lime-rich soils. It has dark, blood-red shoots and the leaves also turn dark red in autumn. It bears clusters of small white flowers and the fruits are small and purplish-black.

Dormancy Inactive state, during which no growth takes place.

Certain animals and many plants and their seeds or spores have periods of dormancy during unfavourable conditions. In some instances dormancy is seasonal, e.g. animal hibernation or the dormancy of bulbs, and forms part of an annual rhythm. In others it only exists for as long as conditions remain unfavourable. A seed, for example, which needs water to germinate, will remain dormant until it is put in moist soil.

Dormouse A small rodent that looks similar to a mouse but behaves more like a squirrel. Dormice have long, often bushy tails and are good climbers. They are active at night and hibernate for several months during the winter. The common or hazel dormouse is the smallest species, no more than 9 cm long. It has a golden brown coat and is found in most of NW Europe except Ireland and the far north. It lives among bushes where it makes a small, ball-shaped nest. Its favourite food is hazelnuts. See also EDIBLE DORMOUSE and GARDEN DORMOUSE.

**Common
dormouse**

Dot moth A common moth recognized by the white spot on each of its dark forewings. The larva of the dot moth is brown to green in

Dot moth
and caterpillar

colour, and eats a variety of plants, including nettles.

Dotterel A bird belonging to the plover family, found on seashores and moorland. It nests on the ground, mainly in the far noth, and will pretend to be injured in order to decoy an intruder away from the eggs or chicks. It feeds on snails, grubs, worms and insects.

Dove See PIGEON.

Down Soft, fluffy plumage of new-born birds. Also the under-plumage of certain adult birds, especially water birds, e.g. ducks and geese.

Dragonet One of the most colourful fishes found around European coasts, with tall, sail-like fins. The male has bright blue and gold markings with an extended first ray in the dorsal fin. The female is duller. Dragonets grow up to 30 cm long and live on sandy sea beds.

Dragonfly A group of insects that are among the most efficient aerial hunters. Dragonflies catch other insects on the wing, usually near or over water. They can fly forwards or backwards and can also hover in mid-air. They have excellent eyesight and many species are brightly coloured. The dragonfly nymph lives under water and is an equally fierce predator. See picture on page 60.

Drake A male duck.

Drey A squirrel's nest, built in a tree.

Drone-fly A hover-fly which in flight makes a whining noise. It gets its name from its remarkable similarity to the male honey bee (drone). It is a true fly, which feeds on nectar and pollen from flowers. Drone-fly larvae live at the bottom of ponds, breathing air through a long hose-like tube.

Dryad's saddle A bracket fungus, especially common on elm but also found on many other deciduous trees. The brackets are fan-shaped and scaly, sometimes up to 60 cm across. They often grow in overlapping tiers and may be high up on the trunk. The fungus weakens the tree and often causes the branches to snap off.

Dry rot A fungus that is a serious pest in old, damp buildings where it attacks floor boards and other concealed timbers. The wood becomes clothed with a greyish blanket of fungal threads, and coarse dark strands spread out and carry the infestation to other areas. The fruiting body is a rust-coloured sheet. The whole fungus has a strong musty smell.

Duck A group of birds found worldwide, always close to water. Ducks are related to geese and swans but are smaller with shorter necks and flat beaks. They have webbed feet for swimming and in most species the males and females have very different plumages. There are two main groups of ducks: those which feed on the surface of the water, and those which dive. Surface-feeding ducks, also called dabbling ducks, prefer shallow, inland water and can often be seen up-ended, feeding on water plants. They include the MALLARD, SHOVELER and TEAL. The diving ducks prefer deeper water and several species can be found in coastal waters. They swim beneath the surface of the water to feed on water plants and animals. They include the EIDER, MERGANSER and POCHARD.

Duckweed A group of small aquatic plants that produce tiny petalless flowers. They have no stems or leaves but consist of a leaf-like organ or thallus that floats on the surface of still, fresh water, often forming a carpet. Each thallus has a small rootlet attached to it. Duckweed is commonly eaten by both ducks and fishes.

Dulse A common red seaweed with a branching, fan-shaped frond. It often grows on other seaweeds instead of attaching itself to stones. Certain dulses are edible.

Dung beetle A group of beetles that live on animal dung, both eating it and laying their eggs on it to provide food for their larvae. They often bury the dung before laying their eggs in it. The SCARAB BEETLES are dung beetles.

Dung beetle

Dung-fly A group of insects which lay their eggs in fresh animal dung. A familiar species is the common yellow dung-fly. Large numbers of

Dung-fly

the males can often be seen flying around fresh cowpats, awaiting the females. The females lay their eggs in the cowpat, and the larvae feed on the dung.

Dunlin A small wading bird. In winter its plumage is grey and white, changing to reddish-brown with a black patch on the belly in summer. Dunlins are the commonest small waders, found swimming to find food in the water as well as wading on mud flats.

Dunnock

Dunnock A small sparrow-like bird, the only north European member of a group of birds called accentors. It is also known as the hedge sparrow. It can be distinguished from the true sparrows by its grey underparts and slim beak. It also tends to go about on its own rather than in flocks. Hedge sparrows nest in hedges and bushes and eat insects and seeds.

Dutch elm disease Disease attacking all species of elm. The presence of a certain fungus results in the sap-carrying vessels of the branches becoming blocked. The flow of water and minerals to the leaves is cut off and the tree dies. The fungus is carried from one tree to another by a small bark beetle, which tunnels under the bark to lay its eggs.

E

Eagle Large birds of prey. The eagles are superb fliers, soaring at great heights, with keen eyesight to spot their prey. Eagles kill by striking with their powerful talons (claws), using their hooked bills to tear the flesh. The eagle family includes the golden eagle, sea eagle and bald eagle. Most eagles prefer open mountain country; in Britain they are restricted to the Highlands of Scotland.

Eaglet A young eagle.

Ear shell See ORMER.

Earth A fox's burrow.

Earthball, common A stalkless, spherical fungus similar to puffballs with a slightly flattened top and a thick scaly rind. Yellowish at first, it becomes brown and cracked when ripe, releasing clouds of purplish-black spores through the cracks. It is commonly found growing on sandy ground.

Earth-star Member of a group of fungi comprising a spherical spore chamber supported by a star-shaped base. Earth-stars are simple spheres at first, but the outer skin soon splits into several flaps which usually fold back to form the star. They often curl under at the tips and push the spore chamber up above the ground litter. The spores are released by the action of falling leaves or raindrops. They escape through a small hole at the top of the papery spore chamber.

Earthworm A large group of about 2500 species of annelid worm that burrow in the ground. Earthworms eat their way through the soil, leaving behind unwanted remains as 'casts'. By doing this they help to drain the soil and supply it with air. Earthworms are blind and come to the surface usually at dusk. They are hermaphrodite, each worm having both male and female reproductive organs.

Earwig A group of insects with pincers on their rear end; the pincers are curved in the male, straight in the female. Some earwigs can fly, but rarely do so, usually hiding away in dark places during daylight. At night they come out to feed, scavenging on dead insects and plant matter. The female earwig cares for her young until they can fend for themselves.

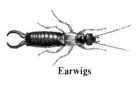

Earwigs

Echinoderm Member of a group of marine invertebrates with radially symmetrical bodies – i.e. the limbs and organs are arranged regularly around a central point. The group includes the sea urchins, starfishes, sea cucumbers and brittlestars. Echinoderms have no brains and no distinctive head, and the skin is embedded with chalky plates that give it a rough appearance. The animals have a unique system of water-filled canals running through their bodies, called a water vascular system. The canals end in small projections on the skin surface called tube-feet. By pumping water through the system the organisms create suction in the tube-feet; this helps them to adhere to rocks or to move about. Tube-feet are also used for respiration. Echinoderm larvae form part of marine plankton.

Ecology Study of the relationships between plants and animals and their environment, including how organisms interact with each other and with their physical (inanimate) surroundings. Ecology involves studying the balances that need to be maintained in order to keep an environment stable.

Ecosystem A given environment, e.g. pond or wood, including all the plants and animals associated with it and their interaction.

Edible dormouse The largest of the dormice, 16 cm long, with a long bushy tail. It is found in most of central and southern Europe, living in gardens and woodlands. The Romans used to fatten it up to eat.

Edible dormouse

Edible frog Either of two similar species of green frog found in central and southern Europe. It is about 12 cm long and spends much of its time in the water, or sunning itself on the bank. It is a noisy creature that croaks both day and night.

Eel, European A long slim fish that migrates from fresh water to the sea to breed. The male grows up to 50 cm long, the female up to 1 metre. Eels spawn in the Sargasso Sea in the western Atlantic Ocean. The leaf-like larvae drift across the Atlantic to Europe, taking up to

Eel

three years to do so. Just before they enter European rivers they change into elvers, young eels. Males stay in inland waters for up to 12 years, and females stay for up to 24 years, before they begin their 4000-km journey back to the Sargasso Sea. Here they spawn and, soon after, die. See also CONGER EEL.

Eel-grass Several species of grass-like marine plants, unique among flowering plants in that they can grow while completely submerged in seawater. They have long slim leaves and tiny green petalless flowers.

Eelpout A fish belonging to the blenny family. It lives on the sea bed in shallow waters and is also found in brackish water. It grows up to 50 cm long and has green bones. The female gives birth to live young.

Egret Heron-like birds, most of which are white. They live mainly in marshes or around lakes, and feed on frogs, small fishes and other water animals. They are found mostly in warmer climates but the little egret (which likes dry grass-land) visits northern Europe.

Eider A duck which spends its time at sea and which is famed for the

male   female

Eider ducks

softness of its feathers or down. The male common eider is black and white, the female being brown. The eider is an excellent swimmer, diving to the seabed to catch crabs, mussels and other shellfish.

Elder A deciduous shrub or small tree belonging to the honeysuckle family. It has clusters of white flowers and juicy black berries that are frequently used for making wine. The bark is thick and soft and the leaves have several leaflets.

Elk Largest of all the deer, standing nearly 2 metres high at the shoulder. It lives among the pine forests of Scandinavia and Finland, and all the way round the Arctic Circle. In North America it is called the moose. The antlers of the male emerge almost horizontally from the head and have a broad flat area from which the points rise. Besides the leaves of trees, elks also eat water plants, and can swim well in order to reach them. They tend to lead solitary lives. See picture on page 142.

Elm A family of deciduous trees that were once very common until, in the 1960s and '70s, millions of them were killed by DUTCH ELM DISEASE. Elms have clusters of small red flowers which open long before the leaves and produce small fruits, each surrounded by a thin wing. Four main species of elm grow in Europe. The English elm is found only in Britain and parts of France. It is a high, narrow tree, about 30 metres tall, with small, hairy leaves. The wych elm may reach up to 40 metres, and has larger and rougher leaves. The smooth-leaved elm is the elm most commonly found in continental Europe. A cross between this and the wych elm is called the Dutch elm.

English elm

Wych elm

Elver A young eel.
Elytron Modified forewing of beetles forming a tough cover over the hind wing.

Embryo (1) A young plant still enclosed in its seed. (2) A young animal still in its egg or, in species which give birth to live young, at an early stage of development inside the mother's body.
Emerald moth A group of moths which, for a short while after emerging from the pupa, are vivid green; later, the colour fades and the moths look grey-blue. The larva of the large emerald looks like a twig; it hibernates on a branch throughout the winter.
Emigration See MIGRATION.

Emperor moth

Emperor moth A heath and woodland moth with a conspicuous 'eye' spot on each of its wings. The rich brown male is smaller than the greyer female. He finds his mate by his astonishingly keen sense of smell.
Engraver beetle See BARK BEETLE.
Entomology The study of insects.
Environment Surroundings of an organism, including both physical and climatic conditions, and other organisms.
Ermine See STOAT.
Ermine moth A group of moths related to the tiger moths. They are mostly white with black markings, named for their similarity to ermine fur. The buff ermine has yellow wings.
Euglena A group of aquatic single-celled organisms that are on the

border line between plants and animals. Because most can photosynthesize, they are more commonly classed as plants, though they are mobile and can also feed like primitive animals. Euglena propel themselves through the water with a whip-like organ called a flagellum. They often form scum on the surface of lakes and ponds.

Evergreen A plant that bears leaves throughout the year. Leaves are lost and replaced as part of a continual process. Most conifers are evergreen, as are a small number of broad-leaved trees, e.g. holly and holm oak.

Evolution The process by which organisms gradually change over successive generations, resulting in better adaptation to the environment and eventually producing new species. The driving force behind evolution is NATURAL SELECTION, i.e. the survival of the fittest. Evolution is believed to account for all the species now in existence, with each group of animals having a common ancestor. The theory of evolution by natural selection was put forward by the naturalist Charles Darwin in 1859, and also (independently) by Alfred Russel Wallace.

Exoskeleton The external skeleton of various animals, including the CUTICLE of arthropods and the shell of molluscs.

Eye-bright Several species of herb related to the foxglove. The well-branched stem supports a leafy spike of two-lipped flowers. The petals are white or purple, often with purple or yellow markings. The plants are semi-parasitic, their roots taking nourishment from those of grasses and other plants. They grow in fields and meadows.

Eyrie The nest of a bird of prey, especially an eagle, built high up on a rock face.

F

Facet See COMPOUND EYE.

Fairy ring A ring of dark, lush grass in meadows and on lawns, caused by various kinds of mushrooms and toadstools growing in the soil. At certain times of the year the toadstools themselves grow up and form a conspicuous ring. The lush grass develops because the fungal threads break down the humus in the soil, releasing nitrogen-rich substances that act as fertilizers. Just inside the lush ring there is a zone of stunted grass. This is where the fungal threads are at their densest and where the toadstools actually spring up. The ring gets bigger each year because the fungal threads keep pushing outwards. They cannot grow back towards the centre because they have exhausted all the food in the inside of the ring. Rings of toadstools can be found in the woods as well as on grassland.

Horse mushroom

Fairy shrimp Freshwater crustaceans with transparent bodies and many legs. Their legs are used for swimming, to catch food, and as gills for breathing. Because the eggs may live out of water for years, fairy shrimps may suddenly appear in newly-formed pools.

Falcon Birds of prey, related to hawks, but with longer pointed wings and longer tails. Examples are the handsome GYRFALCON, the small KESTREL and the MERLIN. The peregrine falcon, a bird of rocky cliffs, is one of the fastest fliers of all. It dives, or 'stoops', with wings half-folded, to strike its prey (often a pigeon) in mid air.

Fallow deer A native of the Mediterranean region, this is the deer most often found in parks. It stands about 85 cm high at the shoulder and usually has a red-brown summer coat with white spots; the winter coat is duller and darker with less distinct spots. The

Fairy ring

Field
mushroom

mature males have antlers with broad, flat blades. Fallow deer live in large herds and are active day and night, feeding mainly on grass. See picture on page 62.

False foot See PSEUDOPODIUM.

Family One of the main groups in animal and plant CLASSIFICATION. Families are divided into genera containing closely related species.

Fanworm A group of marine bristle worms which live inside tubes made of lime or sand grains. Fanworms filter food from water with a fan of bristles projecting from the end of the tube. The PEACOCK WORM of seashores is a fanworm.

Fat-hen A flowering plant that produces tiny, green, petalless flowers, arranged in alternate spikes up the stem. The leaves are covered in white, bladder-like hairs and the grooved stem is often tinged red. The plant is a goosefoot, and is a common weed of cultivated land.

Fauna The animal life of an area.

Fawn A young deer, up to one year old.

Feather A growth from the skin of birds made up of the horny substance keratin. Feathers form the plumage and probably evolved from reptile scales. They are very important both in flight and in keeping a bird warm. Contour feathers cover a bird's body except for the feet and legs. They consist of a central shaft with a series of branches or barbs growing on each side. The barbs are linked together by a series of hooks called barbules to form a smooth, almost continuous surface. Down feathers are the soft fluffy feathers that cover young birds. They also lie beneath the contour feathers of some adult birds, insulating them from the cold.

Feather-duster worm See PEACOCK WORM.

Featherstar A group of echinoderms

71

that look more like plants than animals. Featherstars have five long arms divided into feathery branches. The central disc is covered in chalky plates and small claws on the underside of the body attach the animal to the sea bed until it is ready to swim away. Featherstars live in calm waters below the low tide level.

Featherstar

Fern A group of green flowerless plants that reproduce by spores. Ferns have roots and a system of vessels for carrying water and food. The plants can therefore grow far larger than the mosses and liverworts. Fern leaves are usually called fronds. They may be quite large and are often divided into many small leaflets. Spores are produced on the underside of the fronds in a series of spore capsules. Once scattered, a spore develops into a small heart-shaped plate called a prothallus. This is the sexual stage of the plant. The union of a male and female sex-cell results in the growth of a new spore-bearing plant. BRACKEN is a typical fern. (See ALTERNATION OF GENERATIONS.)

Fertilization The fusion of a male and female sex-cell during sexual reproduction. It occurs in both animals and plants.

Fescue Name given to a group of grasses, many of which are commonly grown as lawns or pastures or for hay.

Feverfew A fragrant plant related to the daisy. Its well-branched stem supports yellowish leaves and daisy-like flowerheads. The flowerhead is composed of yellow disc FLORETS surrounded by white rays. The plant grows mainly on waste ground and was formerly used as a medicine.

Fieldfare A large member of the thrush family that is often found with redwings. It has a blue-grey back and a mottled breast. Fieldfares breed in Scandinavia and north and central Europe, moving south and west for winter. They make their nests in woodlands and gardens but tend to feed in open farmland and orchards in winter.

Field frog See MOOR FROG.

Field mushroom The common mushroom that people gather in the fields or buy in the shops. The gills are pink at first, turning purplish-brown. The flesh is white but may turn pink on cutting. See picture on page 71.

Field vole

Field vole A vole similar to the common vole in its habits, except that it prefers to live in longer grass because it does not burrow so well. It is found over most of NW Europe except Ireland, often in damp places. Field voles are about 12 cm long and are often active by day.

Fig A group of 600 or so species of broad-leaved tree, related to the mulberries. One deciduous species is grown in Europe for its fruit. It can grow to about 10 metres tall but cultivated trees are generally kept short and grown against south-facing walls for shelter. The fruit is green when unripe, turning a deep purple later. The leaves are very large and rough, and generally divided into five lobes.

Figwort A group of tall flowering plants related to the foxglove. All species have a square stem and clusters of two-lipped flowers. The common figwort produces rust-coloured flowers and is found in wet, woody areas.

Fin Projection on fishes and sea mammals used for swimming and steering. The fins of bony fishes consist of a series of spines or rays linked by a fine layer of skin. Cartilaginous fishes have fins covered in thick, heavy skin. The fins of sea mammals are modified legs.

Finch A large family of seed-eating birds that includes the REDPOLL, LINNET and CROSSBILL, as well as the more common finches. They are mostly colourful birds with strong heavy beaks with which they can crack open the tough cases of seeds. Most of the dozen or so European finches do not migrate, but some of the more northerly birds move further south in winter. See BRAMBLING, BULLFINCH, CHAFFINCH, GOLDFINCH, GREENFINCH, HAWFINCH, SERIN and SISKIN.

Fir Member of a group of 40 or so coniferous trees belonging to the pine family, Firs have flattened needles and woody cones that stand upright. The cones fall to pieces when the seeds are ripe. The trees are widely grown for their timber. The European silver fir grows in the central and southern European mountains. The giant or grand fir was introduced into Europe from western North America in the 1830s. Both trees reach a height of 50 metres. The Douglas fir is not a true

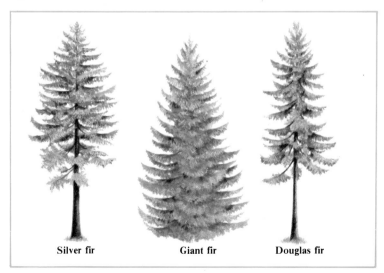

Silver fir   Giant fir   Douglas fir

fir and has cones that hang down. It was discovered in Canada by a Scottish botanist, and brought to Europe. It grows more than 50 metres tall, and its needles smell like lemon.

Firecrest A tiny bird with a bold white strip above the eye and a black-bordered orange crest. It is closely related to the goldcrest, with which it shares the distinction of being the smallest bird in Europe. Firecrests are found only as far north as southern England and southern Denmark. Though they prefer conifers, they also build their nests in other trees.

Firecrest

Fireweed See WILLOWHERB.

Fish An aquatic vertebrate, well adapted to a life in water with, typically, a streamlined body and a series of fins. The two sets of paired fins correspond to the limbs of land animals. Fishes take in oxygen from the water by means of gills. A few species of fish have a form of lung and can breathe air: they are known as lungfishes. Most fishes have scales on the skin and all are cold-blooded – that is, their body temperature is the same as that of their environment. Many species possess a sense apparatus called the LATERAL LINE that is sensitive to pressure and helps the fish detect nearby objects. Some also possess a SWIM-BLADDER to keep them bouyant. There are four basic

groups of fishes: the bony fishes, which include about 95 per cent of all species; the cartilaginous fishes, such as sharks and rays, which have cartilage (gristle) instead of bone; the chimaeras, which are toothless cartilaginous fishes; and the primitive sucking fishes, i.e. the hagfishes and lampreys, which have no jaws – and are also cartilaginous. The gills of bony fishes are protected by a plate called an operculum. Those of the cartilaginous fishes have no such covering and open directly into the water. Bony fishes and jawless fishes have representatives in both fresh and sea water, but the other two groups are found exclusively in the sea. Some fishes, notably the eels and salmon, spend part of their lives at sea and part in fresh water, often migrating many thousands of kilometres to spawn.

Fish hawk See OSPREY.

Flagellate Member of a group of tiny, single-celled animals that move around by means of a whip-like organ called a flagellum. The most familiar flagellate is euglena, which forms green scum on the surface of stagnant ponds.

Flatfish Member of a group of fishes that live at the bottom of the sea. The group includes plaice, dab, flounder, turbot, brill, sole, halibut and several less familiar species such as the topknot, megrim, lemon sole and witch. A flatfish that is only a few weeks old looks much like a herring of the same age. Then it changes: the body flattens and one eye migrates to the other side of the head, so that the fish can lie on the sea floor with both eyes uppermost. Plaice, sole, dab, and halibut lie on the left side, turbot and brill on the right. The upper part of the body of a flatfish is coloured and speckled so that it is hard to detect against the background of the sea bed.

Flatworm Also called platyhelminths, these worms have flat, unsegmented bodies. Some, such as flukes and tapeworms, are parasites living inside other animals; others are free-living, found either in damp places on land or in fresh or salt water. Flatworms are hermaphrodite, that is, both male and female reproductive parts are found on an individual.

Flax A family of slender plants with clusters of blue or white open flowers, mostly five-petalled; commonly found on grasslands.

Flea A group of tiny wingless insects which live as blood-sucking parasites on animals and birds. They can jump quite long distances. Some of the 1600 or so species of flea are specific to one kind of host (such as cats); others are at home on more than one kind of animal. Flea larvae live in the host's nest or home and do not suck blood.

Flea

Fleabane Several species of herb related to the daisy. The blue fleabane is branched towards the top, each branch bearing a solitary flowerhead with yellow disc FLORETS surrounded by purple rays. It is widespread in dry areas. The common fleabane has yellow flowerheads and grows in damp grassy areas.

Flesh-fly A number of true flies, so named because they lay eggs on the bodies of dead animals. The larvae are white, wriggling maggots which feed on the rotting flesh. They then turn into brown pupae from which the adult winged flesh-flies emerge.

Flesh fly

Flora The plant life of an area.

Floret A small flower that forms part of a flowerhead in plants such as dandelions and daisies. The petals are fused to form a tube. There are two types of floret: disc florets and ray florets. A flowerhead may be composed of one or the other or both types. Disc florets are simple tubes, whereas ray florets have one side elongated to form a long strap. Daisies have both types of florets, thistles have discs only and dandelions have rays only.

Flounder A flatfish that lives on the sea bed in inshore waters. It spawns

Flounder

in deep water, but in summer often enters river estuaries and travels upstream. As a rule both eyes are on the right side of the head, but some individuals have the eyes on the left and therefore lie on their right side.

Flower The reproductive part of seed-producing plants. The flowers of coniferous trees are usually referred to as cones. Male and female cones are separate, sometimes borne on different trees.

The flowers borne by true flowering plants, angiosperms, may be single-sexed but usually have both male and female parts. A typical flower has a series of brightly coloured petals called the corolla. Outside the corolla is a ring of green leaf-like structures, or sepals, called the calyx. Together, the calyx and the corolla are known as the perianth. Inside the corolla lie the male parts of the flower – the stamens. These consist of long filaments with pollen-producing bodies called anthers on the end. The female part lies in the centre of the flower and is called the carpel. At the base of the carpel is the ovary containing the egg, or eggs. A projection from the ovary, called the style, ends in a pollen-receiving organ, the stigma. Some flowers have only one carpel, others may have several.

Some flowers also have nectaries at the base of the petals. These contain a sweet substance called nectar that attracts insects to the flower. As they feed on the nectar, the insects deposit pollen picked up from other flowers on the stigmas. This fertilizes the flowers, which then form seeds.

Fluke A group of parasitic flatworms found in a wide range of animals, including humans. Flukes either attach themselves to the outside of their host's body or else live inside the host, sometimes within the blood vessels. There are almost 6000 different species of fluke. One of the commonest is the liver fluke which causes liver rot in sheep. The larval stage of the liver fluke is spent inside a water snail. When the larva emerges it forms a cyst on grass which may subsequently be eaten by a sheep. The fluke then escapes from the cyst and makes its way to the sheep's liver. Eggs pass out with the sheep's droppings and the cycle starts again.

Fly True flies are insects with only a single pair of wings. The second pair have been replaced by pin-like organs called halteres, used for balancing. There are many species of true fly, including fruit-flies, bluebottles, house-flies and mosquitoes. Many feed and lay their eggs on dead animals or decaying plant matter, and some flies carry disease. But by no means are all harmful. The true flies belong to a group of insects called Diptera, meaning 'two-winged'. Several other insects are also called flies but they are not true flies because they are not dipterans.

Greenbottle

House-fly

Thick-headed fly

Pied flycatchers

female

male

Flycatcher Small, broad-beaked birds which make sudden darts from their perches to seize insects on the wing. They build neat cup-shaped nests in any convenient hole, often on buildings. They winter in West Africa. Pied flycatchers haunt woods of oak and ash, often building their nests in woodpeckers' holes. The males have black upper parts and white breasts in the summer, but at other times of the year resemble the females, which are brown with pale underparts. The spotted flycatcher is brown, with dark streaks on its paler head and breast. The bird may be found in parks and gardens.

Food chain A chain of organisms that pass energy from one to the other as each member of the chain feeds on the one below it. For example: a fly feeds on plant material; a spider eats the fly and is in turn eaten by a bird; and the bird is eaten by a fox. The first link in the chain is always a green plant because plants are the only organisms that can make energy-rich food, i.e. sugars. They do this by trapping the energy of sunlight (see PHOTOSYN-THESIS). Food chains rarely have more than five links but they may be interconnected to form complex food webs.

Forget-me-not Several species of low-growing plant belonging to the borage family. They are hairy plants with small, usually blue flowers. The wood forget-me-not bears its vivid blue flowers on long stalks. The water forget-me-not sometimes has pink or white flowers, and is found in very wet places.

Form A hare's lair, or resting place, in the grass.

Fox A carnivore belonging to the dog family. Foxes have long legs with smallish feet, and thick bushy tails. They walk on their toes and are fast runners. The red fox is found throughout Europe and is a cautious, adaptable and intelligent animal. It is about 75 cm long excluding the tail and has a rich, rust-coloured coat. Foxes hunt

Red fox

alone, usually at night, and feed on small animals such as rodents and rabbits. They are common on farms and in woods but many have adapted to life in cities, where they regularly raid dustbins. The smaller Arctic fox lives in the frozen wastes of the Arctic circle and in the mountains of Norway and Sweden. It is 60 cm long and has small ears and a grey-brown coat that turns white in winter.

Foxglove Several species of tall plant related to the figworts and snapdragons. Their tubular blooms are usually pinkish-purple, but may also be white or yellow. They are arranged in long spikes. Foxgloves grow mostly in woodlands. They are poisonous plants and yield the valuable heart drug digitalis.

Fritillary (1) A group of butterflies with mottled orange-yellow wings; the chequered pattern looks like that

of the fritillary flowers. The underwings of many fritillary butterflies are spotted with silver. Examples are the Queen of Spain, marbled, heath and pearl-bordered fritillaries. The group includes some of the most northerly butterflies, several species living well within the Arctic Circle. (2) A short plant related to the lily. Its slender stem bears long grass-like leaves and a solitary, bell-shaped flowerhead. The petals are varying shades of purple and white. The plant is found in damp grassland.

Frog A tailless amphibian with long hind legs used for jumping and swimming. Frogs belong to the same group as toads, the main difference between them being that frogs have smooth skins and toads have rough ones: the division is not a scientific one. Some frogs and toads live permanently in water, and breathe through their skins. But the majority live mostly on land, returning to the water to lay their eggs. These hatch into tadpoles, tiny legless larvae with tails, and gills with which they can breathe. Gradually the tadpoles develop legs and lungs, and lose their tails and gills. After about twelve weeks they look like small adults and are ready to leave the water. The common frog is found in all parts of NW Europe. It is 10 cm long and varies in colour from grey to russet. At mating time the males croak in chorus. See also MARSH FROG, MOOR FROG and EDIBLE FROG.

Frogbit An aquatic plant that floats freely at the surface of fresh water. It has white flowers with yellow markings at the centre. In winter the plant stays on the bottom of the pond in the form of a bud.

Froghopper A family of small jumping bugs whose nymphs produce a frothy spit-like liquid called cuckoo-spit. This froth keeps the larvae moist and also hides them from predators. There are over 2000 species of froghopper, other names for which are cuckoo-spit insect and spittlebug. They leap like frogs and some look like tiny brown frogs.

Common frogs

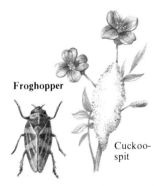

Froghopper

Cuckoo-spit

Frond The leaf of a fern, or the leaf-like part of a seaweed.

Fruit The seed-containing body of flowering plants, formed by the ovary. There are many different types of fruit. Some are dry, such as nuts, the winged fruit of sycamores, or the ripe pods of peas. Others are fleshy, like plums and berries. A few fruits, such as the strawberry, are called false fruits because the main body of the fruit has developed from the receptacle of the flower rather than the ovary.

Fruit-fly Small yellowish-brown flies often found feeding on rotting fruit. They have a short life cycle. Most fruit-fly larvae also feed on rotting vegetable matter.

Fruiting body The spore-producing structure of certain fungi, made up of many tightly-packed threads or hyphae. Mushrooms and toadstools are both examples of fruiting bodies.

Fry Young fishes.

Fulmar A gull-like, grey and white sea bird related to the shearwater. The fulmar nests in colonies on rocky sea cliffs. It is a superb flier, swooping over the waves with only an occasional beat of its wings. Fulmars feed on carrion and fish.

Fumitory A family of plants, mostly rather floppy, with much-divided leaves and tubular flowers. They are often found on arable fields and waste ground.

Fungus Member of a large group of flowerless plants that contains the mushrooms, toadstools, puffballs, moulds and yeasts among many others. They have no leaves and there is never any of the green colour (chlorophyll) found in most other plants. The bulk of the body consists of a mass of fine threads, called hyphae, which spread through or over the food material, e.g. dead plant matter, and absorb nutrients from it. The toadstools that we actually see are the reproductive parts of the fungi – the fruiting bodies, usually produced only at certain times of the year. They consist of densely packed and entwined hyphae. They do not produce seeds like the flowering plants, but scatter millions of tiny spores which are usually carried away by the wind. The simplest fungi, such as pin moulds, carry their spores in little capsules on the hyphae and produce no special fruiting bodies. Many toadstools have spore-bearing gills on the underside of the cap. The colour of the gills and the way in which they are attached to the stalk is important in identifying many species.

Furniture beetle

Furniture beetle A small brown beetle which lays its eggs on timber, often attacking timber in houses. The larvae (woodworms) bore into the wood on which they feed. When fully developed, they pupate just beneath the surface of the wood, and in time the adult beetles emerge chewing their way out. Their exits are the familiar woodworm holes seen in old timber.

G

Gall Abnormal growth of a plant caused by certain insects, mites or fungi. The oak-apple is a common example: it is caused by a gall wasp.

Gall wasp A family of insects which look more like ants than wasps. The larvae live inside plants, causing knobby swellings called galls. Many different kinds affect oak trees, where one of the commonest galls is the oak-apple. Another type of gall, commonly found on wild roses, is called the robin's pin-cushion.

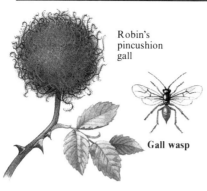

Robin's
pincushion
gall

Gall wasp

Game Certain animals commonly hunted for sport and food, including hares, pheasants and grouse.

Gander A male goose.

Gannet A sea bird which fishes spectacularly by diving into the water from the air. The gannet is a large bird, almost completely white save for dark wing tips and a yellowish patch on the head. Colonies of gannets nest on rocky cliffs, the single egg being laid in a rough nest of grass and seaweed.

Gaper A bivalve mollusc which cannot close its shells completely, hence the name 'gaper'. Gapers live in sand burrows and reach up with long siphon tubes to collect oxygen and food from the water above.

Garden dormouse A large dormouse, up to 17 cm long, found in

Garden dormouse

most of Europe except Britain and Scandinavia. It spends more time on the ground than other dormice and its tail is less bushy. It makes a variety of growling and whistling noises.

Garden snail A land snail which is particularly common in man-made habitats, especially gardens. It has a mottled brown spiral shell, up to 4 cm across. In winter the snail hibernates, sealing its shell with a plug of mucus which hardens into a parchment-like seal. Garden snails feed on plants and are considered to be pests by gardeners.

Garden spider A common web-spinner that has a brown body with a white cross on its back. It traps flies and other small insects in the sticky threads of its wheel-shaped web. Then it paralyses the victim with its venomous fangs, wraps it in silk and later feeds on the body juices.

Garden warbler A dull-coloured little bird that, despite its name, likes scrubland and the edges of woodland rather than gardens. It has a rich song, and migrates to Africa in winter.

Garfish A marine shoaling fish, up to 80 cm long, related to the flying fishes of tropical seas. Also known as the garpike, it has a long slim body with long narrow jaws and its bones are turquoise-green. It is often found with shoals of mackerel.

Garlic mustard A hairless flowering plant related to the cabbage. The slender stem bears long-stalked leaves which smell of garlic. The small white flowers are arranged in a cluster at the tip. The plant is found on waste ground and in hedges.

Garpike See GARFISH.

Gastropod Member of a group of molluscs that includes slugs, snails, limpets and whelks. Many live in the sea, though there are freshwater and land forms; and most possess a single, often coiled shell. Gastropods have a distinct head, with eyes and tentacles, and feed by scraping at food material with a file-like structure called a radula. The base of the body consists of a flat, muscular foot.

Gatekeeper A brown butterfly, also known as the hedge brown. Orange-brown in colour, it has 'eye' spots on its wings and is often seen feeding on bramble flowers.

Genet The lithe, agile genet is a relative of the mongoose. Originally from Africa, it is now also found in woodlands in south-west Europe. It eats rodents and birds.

Most species are for this reason named cranesbills or storksbills.

Germination The early growth of a seed that results in a new plant. The process requires moisture and warmth before it can proceed. First the seed swells up with water until the seed-coat bursts open. Then a root, or radicle, emerges and begins to grow downwards into the soil. Finally the young shoot or plumule

Genet

Gentian A group of hairless flowering plants, common to colder regions and mountains, with blue, purple or yellow bell-shaped flowers. The spring gentian forms low tufts on the ground and produces blue star-shaped flowers. The great yellow gentian has large clusters of starry yellow blooms. All the gentians favour damp, boggy places.

Genus One of the main groupings used in animal and plant CLASSIFICATION. Each genus contains a number of closely related species.

Geometer A family of moths which include the carpet and emerald moths. The caterpillar of a geometer moth moves in a looping manner, for it has legs only at the front and rear of its body. This motion led to the larva being given names such as looper and, because it appears to be measuring, measuring worm or inch worm.

Geranium A family of flowering plants, often with aromatic leaves, whose fruit ends in a pointed beak.

begins to grow upwards towards the light.

Gestation period The period between fertilization and birth in mammals. In mice it can be as little as three weeks, and in elephants as long as twenty-two months.

Gill (1) Structure by which many aquatic animals are able to breathe in water. Fishes have internal plates of gills at the side of the head. The gills are well supplied with blood and, as water passes over them, oxygen passes easily from the water into the blood. Carbon dioxide passes in the opposite direction. Other animals, including various young insects and young tadpoles, have feathery external gills. Those of the tadpoles grow outwards from the side of head; they are usually replaced by internal gills after a while. Many molluscs and crustaceans also have gills. (2) Spore-bearing structure on the underside of the cap of certain mushrooms and toadstools.

Ginkgo A deciduous tree also called the maidenhair tree, and the only living representative of a group of trees that flourished millions of years ago. Native to China, it is commonly grown in Europe as an ornamental tree. The leaves are heart-shaped, and male and female flowers are borne on separate trees. The fruit is small and fleshy, and smells unpleasant.

Gladiolus, wild A flowering plant belonging to the iris family. The deep-red flowers are borne in a spike on the leafless stem. The sword-shaped leaves grow from the root. In Britain they are found wild only in the New Forest. There are other species occurring as garden escapes.

Glasswort An unusual-looking plant belonging to the goosefoot family. It is a small fleshy plant with tiny green flowers that barely resemble flowers at all. Its leaves are scale-like and envelop the stem which may be tinged red or yellow. There are several species, commonly found in saltmarshes.

Globe flower A flowering plant related to the buttercup. The large flowers have no petals, but the 10 yellow sepals curve inwards at the tip, forming a globe. Globe flowers are found in damp fields.

Globularia Several species of short flowering plant often found on mountains. Globularia have mostly

Matted globularia

blue, almost spherical flowerheads made up of many tiny two-lipped flowers.

Glow-worm Beetles related to the fireflies of Southern Europe. The male has wings, but the wingless female spends her life on the ground. It is she who is the 'glow-worm', for she can give out a light to attract passing males looking for a mate. The light is a cold one, similar to that

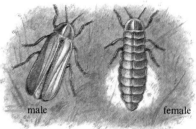

male   female

Glow-worms

produced by a fluorescent tube, and is caused by a chemical reaction.

Glutton See WOLVERINE.

Gnat A name loosely used for a wide variety of slender flies, especially some of those that dance up and down in swarms. The blood-sucking MOSQUITOES are often called gnats, but not all gnats suck blood. Many do not feed at all in the adult state. Some grow up in the water, while others spend the larval stage in fungi or in decaying matter. See also MIDGE.

Goatsbeard A flowering plant of the daisy family, otherwise known as Jack-go-to-bed-at-noon because the solitary yellow flowerheads only open fully on sunny mornings. The leaves are grass-like and the tufted seeds form a large 'clock'. The plant grows on dry, waste ground.

Goatsucker See NIGHTJAR.

Goby Member of a group of small and rather spiny fishes which live in

Goby

coastal waters or rivers. Their
ventral fins are joined to form a
sucker with which they can cling to
stones. The common goby lives in
rock pools and in brackish estuaries.
It is about 7 cm long.

Godwit Wading birds, larger than
most other waders, with a long bill
that curves upwards at the tip. The
plumage is mottled reddish-brown
in summer, greyish-white in winter.
The black-tailed and bar-tailed
godwit live on seashores.

Goldcrest A tiny bird which, along
with its close relative the firecrest, is
Europe's smallest bird, weighing

Goldcrest

only 5 g. It has a greyish-green
plumage, and a black-bordered crest
which is orange in the male and
yellow in the female. Goldcrests
make their tiny nests in conifers,
both in forests and gardens.

Goldeneye Bay ducks of northern
regions, mainly black with white
wing patches. Goldeneye are fast in
flight, and good divers.

Golden oriole A bright, black and
yellow bird, a little larger than a song
thrush; the female is green and
black. It is a summer visitor to most
of Europe. Orioles usually hang

their nests from high, forked
branches. They feed on insects, but
take fruit when in season, especially
figs.

Golden-rod A flowering plant of the
daisy family. Its flowerheads are
bright yellow and borne in branched
spikes. The leaves are oval near the
base of the stem, becoming narrower along the stem itself. The
plant is found in grassy and heathy
areas.

Goldfinch

Goldfinch A bird much beloved by
farmers and gardeners, not just
because of its pretty plumage but
because it eats the seeds of thistles,
burdock and other weeds. It is
readily recognized by the red patch
on its face and the wide yellow wing
bars. Goldfinches are commonly
found in parks, gardens and
orchards as well as woodlands and
hedgerows.

Gold tail See YELLOW-TAIL MOTH.

Goosander A large duck found on
seashores, river estuaries and lakes.
The male is glossy green-black
above, with pinky-white underparts.
The female is grey above, with a
brown head. The goosander swims
under water to catch fish; its slender
bill has serrated edges to grip the fish
securely.

Goose Large birds related to ducks
and swans. Geese are usually found
near water, although they generally
feed on land (by grazing). They have

White-fronted goose

Pink-footed goose

Brent goose

webbed feet and swim well, though they rarely dive. Geese often live in large flocks and make long migratory flights, flying in V-formations called skeins. Examples of geese are the BARNACLE GOOSE, GREYLAG GOOSE and CANADA GOOSE.

Gooseberry A small spiny shrub related to the currant. It produces green flowers and a green, usually hairy fruit which is edible.

Goosefoot A group of flowering plants with inconspicuous, green, petalless flowers arranged in spikes. They are weeds of cultivated land and are often found near the sea. The FAT-HEN is the most common species.

Goosegrass See CLEAVERS.

Gordian worm See HAIRWORM.

Goshawk A bird of prey, similar to the sparrow-hawk but larger. It is a bird of northern woodlands, hunting small birds and mammals. As with most hawks, the female is larger than the male.

Gosling A young goose.

Gossamer Light web material spun by certain spiders, often seen floating through the air.

Grass The grasses form one of the largest families of the flowering plants. They have long thin leaves and tiny petalless green flowers that grow in spikes. Grasses grow almost everywhere. They include cereals such as wheat, barley and oats.

Grasshopper A group of jumping insects, related to crickets and locusts, with long, powerful hind

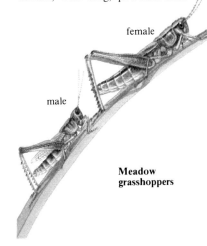

female

male

Meadow grasshoppers

legs. Some of them can fly. Grasshoppers are active on warm, sunny days and are noted for their 'song' (called stridulation) which they produce by rubbing their hind legs against their wings. Grasshoppers feed on grasses and other plants.

Grass-of-Parnassus A short flowering plant with a rosette of heart-shaped leaves at the base of its stem and solitary white flowers. It is found in wet, marshy places.

Grass snake A snake commonly found in damp places over most of Europe except the extreme north and Ireland. It is 1.2 metres long and usually has distinct yellow and black markings on the neck. It is not poisonous but hisses and pretends to strike if it is cornered.

Great diving beetle

Grass snake

Grayling (1) A slender freshwater fish related to the salmon. It grows up to 50 cm long and has a tall fin on its back. Its flesh has a thyme-like smell. The fish lives in cool, quick-flowing rivers, feeding on insect larvae. (2) A brown butterfly, mottled on its undersides, making it hard to spot when resting.

Great diving beetle A fierce water beetle which preys on other fresh-water animals including tadpoles and small fishes. The beetle larva

breathes by sticking the end of its body up above the surface of the water.

Great tit The largest member of the tit family. It has a black head with white cheeks and a black stripe running down the centre of its yellow chest. The bird's song, 'teacher, teacher', is distinctive but is only part of a large vocabulary. Great tits nest in holes and readily take to nesting-boxes. See picture on page 172.

Grebe Birds similar to the diver. Grebes live in fresh water, diving to feed on fishes, water insects and shellfish. Some species have boldly marked heads with ear tufts and crests, and in the mating season they perform a courtship dance across the surface of the water, rushing to and fro in an almost upright position. The adults carry their chicks on their backs until the young are ready to swim. The great crested grebe nests on a floating raft of plants. The grebe family also includes the smaller red-necked grebe and the little grebe or dabchick.

Greenbottle Several large flies, similar to the bluebottles, but with metallic-green bodies. They usually lay their eggs on carrion but sometimes choose live animals; one species for instance attacks sheep.

male

Greenfinches

female

Greenfinch A bird frequently seen in parks and gardens where it likes to nest in cypresses and other evergreens. It has a predominantly green plumage with a yellowish rump and bright yellow markings on the wings. Though not so agile as tits, they too can feed from bags of nuts hung out in the garden.

Greenfly See APHID.

Green laver See SEA-LETTUCE.

Green lizard A lizard found over most of southern and central Europe but absent further north. It is about 40 cm long including the tail, and both sexes are bright green. It lives in dry, bushy areas where it climbs, and hunts mostly insects.

Greenshank See REDSHANK.

Green woodpecker A colourful woodpecker with bright green upper parts and a red crown. It is a permanent resident over most of Europe except Ireland and northern Scandinavia. With their long tongues, green woodpeckers frequently feed on ants, and may be seen pecking on lawns. They are not often heard drumming on wood, but their laughing cry has earned them the nickname of 'yaffle'.

Greylag goose A large, very common goose that lives in flocks on moors and marshes. It feeds on grain and grass. The greylag goose has a greyish-brown plumage with a pale grey rump, and its bill and legs are pinkish-orange. It is the ancestor of all domestic geese.

Grisette, tawny A woodland toadstool that first pushes through the soil like a large, brown acorn, but

Green lizard

the cap soon flattens out. It can usually be recognized by the slightly ribbed margin. The gills are white and there is a ragged cup or bag at the base of the stalk.

Grosbeak Birds belonging to the finch family with large cone-shaped beaks for eating seeds. The scarlet grosbeak lives in north-east Europe; the pine grosbeak is found from Siberia to Scandinavia. It is the largest European finch.

Ground beetle A large group of beetles which run over the ground, seldom taking wing. Most are hunters and are active at night. The violet ground beetle, found in gardens, preys on other insects and worms. The large green ground beetle climbs trees to hunt caterpillars.

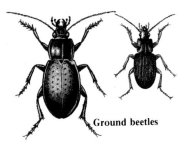
Ground beetles

Ground elder A low-growing weed related to the carrot. It produces clusters of tiny white flowers and forms patches on wasteground.

Ground hopper A group of small insects similar to grasshoppers and also known as grouse locusts. Unlike grasshoppers they do not sing.

Ground ivy A low-growing fragrant plant with mostly purple flowers arranged in whorls at the base of the broad leaves. It is found in woodlands and hedges.

Groundsel Several species of flowering plant related to the daisy. The common groundsel produces yellow flowerheads composed of tiny florets. The heads are usually tight and bud-like and are surrounded by sepal-like bracts. Groundsel is a common weed of cultivated land and wasteground.

Grouse Game birds, often reared on moors specifically for shooting. Grouse are stout birds which spend most of their time on the ground, only taking wing when alarmed. The red grouse and black grouse are common moorland species. The PTARMIGAN of the northern tundra changes to a white plumage in winter.

Grouse locust See GROUND HOPPER.

Grub Term commonly applied to worm-like insect larvae, particularly those found in the soil.

Gudgeon A small freshwater fish belonging to the carp family, found all over Europe except the extreme north and south. It prefers fast-running streams, but is also found in lakes and slower rivers. It has two barbels on its jaws and grows up to 20 cm long.

Guelder rose A deciduous shrub, about 4 metres tall, related to the elder. It produces clusters of white flowers. The showy outer flowers are not fertile, but lure insects to the dull inner ones. The lobed leaves are similar to maple leaves. The fruits are bright red and very bitter.

Guelder rose

Common gull

Herring gull

Guillemot A seabird belonging to the auk family. The guillemot is a true ocean-dweller, seldom coming ashore except to breed. It is a dark-brown bird with a white breast, has webbed feet, and swims and dives with ease to catch fishes. Guillemots lay their single eggs on rocky ledges, high up on sea cliffs; the egg is pear-shaped, and so less likely to roll off.

Gull A group of medium to large seabirds with black, grey and white plumages. They are familiar birds of the seashore, making raucous cries as they squabble for scraps of food.

Gulls eat animal food when they can get it, but are not good at catching fish. They are scavengers and are commonly found near human habitation. Some travel inland to visit ploughed fields or gardens in search of worms and insects.

Gulls nest in colonies on cliffs or on the ground. At least 14 species are found around European coasts. The common gull is similar in appearance to the HERRING GULL but has yellow legs and no red spot on the underside of its bill. Despite its name

it is not the commonest gull; the herring and the BLACK-HEADED GULL are far more numerous. See also BLACK-BACKED GULL, and KITTIWAKE.

Gunnel See BUTTERFISH.

Gurnard Any of several species of marine fish found in coastal waters. Gurnards have three pairs of fin-rays beneath the head which they use as feelers, and even for 'tiptoeing' along the sea bed. They 'talk' to each other by grunting.

Gymnosperm Member of a group of seed-bearing plants that bear their seeds exposed, usually on cones, rather than enclosed within fruits. The group includes the conifers.

Gypsy moth A tussock moth which lives in deciduous trees. Only the tan-coloured males fly, sometimes in large groups. The paler females live on tree bark, laying their eggs in crevices. The larvae feed on many kinds of trees.

Gyrfalcon Largest of the falcons, this handsome bird of prey lives on the treeless tundra plains of the northern hemisphere. It is a fast flier, and its main prey are other tundra birds, such as the ptarmigan.

H

Habitat A plant's or an animal's natural environment, such as woodland, fresh water, or seashore.

Haddock A marine fish belonging to the cod group and easily recognizable by the large black spot above the pectoral fin. It has three dorsal fins which can grow up to 1 metre long, though it is generally somewhat shorter. Haddock live close to the sea bed around the European coast, at depths of up to 200 metres, and spawn in the North Sea.

Hagfish A primitive fish (cyclostome) with an eel-like body and a sucking mouth with no jaws. A series of barbels surround the mouth and nostrils. Hagfishes live close to the sea bed, up to 800 metres deep. They are blind but have a good sense of smell. They eat other animals, boring into the flesh of other fishes.

Hair Only mammals have the pigmented strands of dead cells, growing from beneath the skin, that are called hairs. Other animals may have bristles made of chitin.

Hairstreak A group of butterflies named after the white hair-like streak on the underside of the wings. They are mostly brown, but with orange, blue or purple wing markings in some species. The green hairstreak is brown above, but green beneath, so that it looks like a different butterfly altogether when at rest with its wings folded. The purple hairstreak is a woodland butterfly, commonly found around oaks.

Hairworm About 250 species of long thin worms, also called gordian worms. Young hairworms live as parasites inside crabs and other water-living animals. The adults live freely in sea or fresh water, looking like strands of brown cotton caught up in the water plants. Some can be up to a metre long.

Hake A marine fish belonging to the cod group. It is a fierce hunter in coastal waters, living during the day near the sea bed at depths of up to

Purple hairstreak and underside

Green hairstreak and underside

Green-spot hairstreak and underside

300 metres and rising closer to the surface at night to hunt fishes such as herrings, mackerel and sprats. It grows up to 1 metre long.

Halibut The giant of the flatfishes, growing up to 3 metres long. It lives at depths of up to 2000 metres and feeds on small fishes. Halibut live up to 50 years.

Haltere Modified hind wing of the true flies, used to help maintain balance during flight.

Hare A mammal closely related to the rabbit but easily distinguished by its long hind legs and ears. Two species are commonly found in Europe. The brown hare lives in open grassy country, resting by day in a form – an area of flattened grass. It measures about 65 cm in length. Brown hares are solitary animals except in spring, when they rush around in groups or stand up and 'box' with one another. The blue or mountain hare tends to live in areas not inhabited by brown hares, in northern Europe and the Alps. It is only about 55 cm long.

Harebell A common flowering plant of the bellflower family. The thin stem bears delicate blue bell-shaped flowers on the end of hair-like stalks. Harebells are known as bluebells in Scotland and flourish on heaths and grasslands.

Harrier Birds of prey belonging to the hawk family, with long slender wings and a graceful flight. They can usually be seen flying low over open country in search of small animals.

Harvestman Over 3000 species of arachnids are known as harvestmen. The name reflects their long, scythe-like legs as well as their abundance in fields in late summer. They share with the CRANE-FLY the nickname Daddy-long-legs.

Harvest mouse Europe's smallest mouse, only 6.5 cm long. It is found nearly everywhere, making its home mostly in cereal crops or long grass. Harvest mice are light enough to climb grass stems in search of seeds, using their long tails to help them. They also build their nests around the stems.

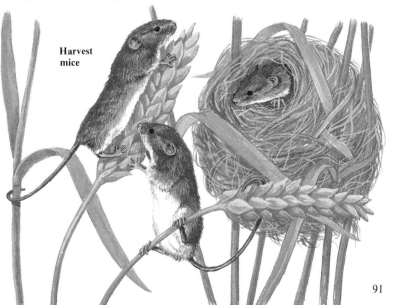

Harvest mice

Hawfinch A member of the finch family with a huge powerful bill which can crack fruit stones such as those of cherries or olives. The birds are particularly fond of hornbeam seeds. Their plumage is chestnut-brown with black wing tips and a black throat. Hawfinches live in

Hawksbeard Several species of flowering plant related to the daisy. They have branched stems bearing yellow dandelion-like flowerheads. The smooth hawksbeard is widespread in grassy areas and on wasteground and grows up to 1 metre tall.

male

Hawfinches

female

woodlands and move south and west in the winter.

Hawkbit Several species of flowering plant related to the daisy, bearing yellow dandelion-like flowerheads. The rough hawkbit is the most common; it is also called the greater hawkbit. All species are commonly found on dry grassland.

Hawk moth Stout, fast-flying moths, most of which fly at night. One of the largest and best-known species is the death's head, which has a skull-like mark on its thorax, just behind the head. The bee-hawks and the humming-bird hawk are smaller moths, which can hover to feed from a flower and dart very rapidly from one bloom to another. Both these moths are day fliers.

Hawkweed A large group of flowering plants with dandelion-like flowerheads. The species are difficult to identify as any one species may have many variants or 'micro-species'. The common hawkweed, for example, has over 200 micro-species. Hawkweeds are found in grassy and rocky places, sometimes up mountains.

Eyed hawk moth

Hawthorn A shrub or small tree related to the rose and also known as may. There are several species, often used for hedging because they are quick-growing and thorny. Hawthorns produce small perfumed flowers (may blossom) which are usually white, but sometimes pink or red. The rich red fruit is known as a haw.

Hazel A deciduous tree related to the birch. Hazels can grow up to 12 metres tall, but are usually cut down to form bushes. The catkins appear before the broad, hairy leaves, and eventually produce nuts which are popular with mice and squirrels as well as people.

Heath A large group of low, evergreen shrubs, including heather, commonly found on heaths and moors. They produce globular or bell-shaped flowers which are purple, pink or white.

Heath See BROWN BUTTERFLY.

Heather See HEATH.

Hedgehog An insectivore found throughout Europe except in northern Scandinavia. It measures 25 cm in length. The hairs of its coat are very thick, with those on the back and sides forming stiff, sharp spines. When in danger, some hedgehogs can roll into a tight prickly ball that few animals are willing to attack. They are nocturnal creatures and hibernate during the winter. They eat many insects, along with slugs, worms, snails, and fruit when in season.

Hellebore A flowering plant of the buttercup family. There are several species. The best known is the stinking hellebore which is found in woods and scrubland. It bears small pale green flowers which become tinged with purple as the plant gets older. The plant gets its name from its nasty smell, and it is highly poisonous.

Helleborine The name given to several species of orchid. Unlike many other orchids, the flowers, which are arranged in a one-sided spike, have no spurs. Many species, such as the broad-leaved and common white helleborines, flourish in woodlands. Others are found in marshes or on dunes. Like many other orchids, some species are becoming increasingly rare.

Hemlock (1) Member of a group of evergreen coniferous trees belonging to the pine family. The western hemlock comes from western North America and is commonly grown for its good strong timber. It gets its name because its soft flat leaves smell like the unrelated poisonous herb hemlock. In Europe it reaches a height of 50 metres, and bears small egg-shaped cones. The eastern hemlock from eastern North America is a much smaller tree, 32 metres high, and is often planted as an ornament. It does not make good timber. (2) A highly poisonous herb

Western hemlock

related to the carrot. It is recognized by its stem which is marked with small purple dots, and its flat-topped clusters of tiny white flowers. It has an unpleasant smell when crushed. The unripe fruit was once used for medicinal purposes. Hemlock grows in moist places such as ditches and damp woods.

Hemp nettle Several species of flowering plant related to the dead-nettle. The common hemp nettle is a weed of cultivated land and has a hairy stem and non-stinging, nettle-like leaves. Its flowers are pink or, less commonly, yellow or white. They are arranged in whorls around the base of the upper leaves.

Henbane An extremely poisonous flowering plant related to the deadly nightshade. Its pale-yellow, purple-veined flowers are arranged in a leafy cluster at the tip of the stem. The stem is hairy and covered in a sticky substance. The plant usually grows on disturbed ground, often by the sea.

Hepatica A short flowering plant of the buttercup family. Its smooth stalks support solitary buttercup-like flowers which are usually deep blue. Its three-lobed leaves are evergreen. The plant is commonly found in woodlands.

Herald moth A moth which flies in late summer and autumn. It looks like an autumn leaf when at rest. During winter, the herald moth hibernates in hollow trees and attics, taking to the wing again in spring.

Herald moth

Herb A flowering plant that has no woody stem and which dies down after flowering. Some other plants used in cookery and medicine, such as rosemary, are also called herbs.

Herbivore A plant-eating animal.

Herb-robert A flowering plant of the geranium family, closely related to the cranesbills. It is of medium height, with a hairy stem and leaves that often turn red. Its five-petalled flowers are pink and the fruits end in a prominent 'beak'. The plants are often found growing among rocks in woodland and in hedgerows.

Heredity The passing on of charac-teristics from parents to offspring.

Hermaphrodite A plant or animal that has both male and female parts on the same individual. Usually, barriers exist to prevent self-fertilization. Certain animals, such as earthworms and many snails, are hermaphrodites; so too are many plants, among which a typical flower has both stamens and carpels.

Hermit crab Unlike most crabs, hermit crabs have no protective shell. They hide their soft bodies in the old shells of other animals such as whelks. When the crab grows too big for its chosen home, it has to find a new one.

Heron Very large water birds with long legs and necks. They stand patiently in shallow water waiting to seize fishes with their long, stabbing bills, sometimes shading the surface with their wings spread. The common or grey heron is found by rivers, lakes and estuaries. It has a grey back and black wing edges, a white head and neck, and a black crest. It is easily recognized in the air by its large wingspan and its slow, flapping flight with the head pulled in to the shoulders. Grey herons nest in colonies, mostly in trees.

Herring One of the most abundant marine fishes found off Europe.

Herring

Herring form huge shoals of many thousands in the open seas. They feed on plankton at night and migrate from place to place. A full grown herring is about 40 cm long.

Herring gull A large seagull, found both on coasts and inland. It has a grey back and wings with black wing-tips, white head and underparts, and pink or yellow legs. The bill is yellow with a red spot on the underside. It is one of the most common and widespread of the gulls, and large flocks of them can often be seen following ploughs on farmland, feeding on the small creatures being churned up. They also eat fish, carrion and the eggs of other birds, and will scavenge through rubbish tips.

Hibernation The period of dormancy undergone by certain animals during the winter to avoid harsh weather conditions and lack of food. During hibernation an animal's metabolism (the internal chemical process) slows right down, and the temperature of warm-blooded creatures drops to that of the environment.

Hind A female deer, particularly red deer.

Hobby A bird of the falcon group, coloured grey above, speckled white and chestnut below. The hobby is smaller than the kestrel, and in flight it glides rather than hovers. It lives in open country with scattered trees, catching small birds and insects.

Hogweed A plant of the carrot family, up to 3 metres high, with a hairy, tough, hollow stem, large rough leaves and a crown of delicate white flowers. The giant hogweed is a taller species; it grows up to 5 metres high, and has a red blotched stem. Hogweed is also known as cow parsnip and is common by waysides.

Holdfast The circular organ at the base of seaweeds by which the plants attach themselves to rocks.

Holly An evergreen shrub or small tree with leathery, glossy green leaves. Those leaves growing in the lower branches are spiny, while those higher up have wavy or even smooth edges. The male and female flowers grow on separate trees which explains why only some trees bear the characteristic scarlet berries.

Holt An otter's lair.

Honey bee A social insect and the best known of all the bees because it is widely bred by bee-keepers for its honey. A hive contains about 60,000 bees of three different kinds: drones, workers, and a queen bee. The queen lays eggs and does little else.

Honey bees

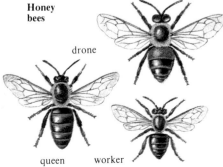

drone

queen   worker

The drones are the males; they are produced late in the season and are needed only to mate with a new queen. Most of the bees are workers, females which cannot lay eggs. They build the wax honeycombs, fetch pollen and nectar to make honey, and look after the queen and young bees. Larvae fed with a special food called royal jelly grow into new queens. The first adult queen to emerge kills off all the other queens and departs on a 'marriage flight' with the drones. After mating she returns to the hive and the old queen either departs with a few workers to set up a new colony, or is killed. Queens can live several years but workers live only a few weeks.

Honey-dew A sweet substance produced by various bugs, such as greenfly, and commonly found coating leaves in summer. It is a popular food of ants, bees and flies; ants can often be seen 'milking' greenfly for their honey-dew.

Honey fungus A common toadstool, appearing in tufts at the bases of trees. It often kills the trees, and then goes on living on the dead trunks. The tan-coloured cap is covered in prominent scales and becomes saucer-shaped with age.

Honeysuckle A deciduous shrub that twines clockwise around any convenient bush or sapling for support. It is characterized by its sweet-smelling blossom; the two-lipped flowers are trumpet-shaped and arranged in a flowerhead, facing outwards from a central point.

Hoopoe One of the most exotic-looking birds found in Europe with its prominent black-tipped crest, black and white barred wings and pinkish-brown head and breast. It is a summer visitor, but is only occasionally seen in the British Isles or Scandinavia.

Horehound Two species of flower-ing plant related to the dead-nettle. The black horehound has whorls of pale purple flowers and an unpleasant smell. The white horehound has downy leaves and stem, and thick whorls of white flowers. It was once used as a cough cure. Both plants are found on wasteland.

Hornbeam A deciduous tree, up to 30 metres tall. It is often mistaken for beech, but can be distinguished from it by its trunk, which is heavily grooved, and also by its toothed leaves. It produces bright yellow catkins and clusters of tiny nuts.

Hornet A large wasp, with a browner body than the familiar black-and-yellow wasp. Like other social wasps, hornets make large communal nests, generally in hollow trees. Unless disturbed, they are not usually aggressive.

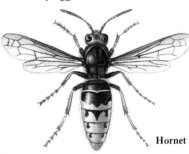

Hornet

Horntail See WOOD WASP.

Hornwrack See SEA MAT.

Horse chestnut A deciduous tree, native to eastern Europe but widely planted elsewhere for ornament and shade. It has long conical clusters of showy white flowers and large, fan-shaped, compound leaves. Its seeds or conkers are born inside spiny cases. Although this fruit is similar in appearance to that of the sweet chestnut, the two trees are not closely related.

Horse chestnut

Horse-fly A group of true flies that make a loud humming noise in flight. The females feed by sucking blood from animals, particularly horses and cattle, and will also bite humans. The male horse-fly does not suck blood but feeds on nectar from flowers. Horse-flies are large, up to 25 mm long.

Horse-fly

Horse-hair fungus A delicate woodland toadstool with a slender, shiny black stalk resembling a horse hair. The cap is brown and wrinkled; the gills are brown. It grows on conifer needles and small twigs, especially heather, in the summer.

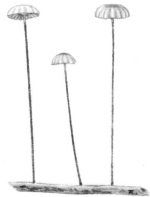

Horse-hair fungus

Horse mushroom A common grassland toadstool that often forms fairy rings in the autumn. The large cap is creamy and the stalk is distinctly swollen at the base. There is a ring on the stem and in the young stages it resembles a cogwheel just under the gills. The gills are white at first, turning purplish brown. See picture on page 70.

Horseradish A tall flowering plant of the cabbage family. It has large, wavy-edged basal leaves and smaller, narrow stem leaves. The delicate white flowers are arranged in long-stalked spikes.

Horseshoe bat Two species of bat are so named because they bear a horseshoe-shaped growth on their noses. The greater horseshoe bat is about 6 cm long and is found only as far north as southern England and south Wales. It hibernates in large numbers in caves, old mines and lofts. The lesser horseshoe bat is

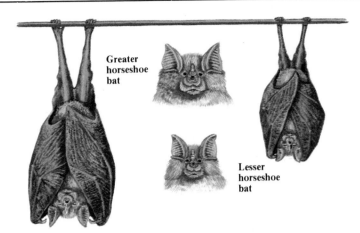

Greater horseshoe bat

Lesser horseshoe bat

found over a wider area than its cousin, including Ireland. It is only 4 cm long and does not hibernate in such dense colonies as the larger species.

Horsetail A group of green flowerless plants which live mainly in damp places. Horsetails are related to ferns. The plants have a system of rhizomes (underground stems). They also have tall ridged stems that snap easily at intervals, where there is a 'joint'. The joints are surrounded by a collar of tiny scale leaves; there are no proper leaves. Spores form in soft cones at the tips of the stems and, when scattered, they form small prothalli like those of the ferns. The prothallus is the sexual phase which gives rise to a new spore-bearing plant. (See ALTERNATION OF GENERATIONS.)

Host A plant or animal that is attacked by a parasite. Most parasites have a specific host, and sometimes two, during their life cycle. For instance, the liver fluke lives first as a larva inside watersnails and later as an adult inside sheep, causing the disease liver-rot.

Houndstongue A flowering plant of the borage family. The common houndstongue is so called because its leaves are long and broad, and resemble a dog's tongue. It has deep red flowers arranged in loose clusters and its flattened spiny fruits cling to clothing and animal fur.

House-fly A true fly which lives in and around houses, feeding on rubbish and human waste. It feeds by spitting on to the food to make a paste which it can then suck up. House-flies spread diseases, since they move constantly from dung and decaying matter to fresh food. The eggs are laid in dung or rubbish, and hatch into white maggots. There are several similar species.

House-fly

Houseleek Several species of flowering plant belonging to the stonecrop

family. The houseleek is a fleshy
plant. At the very tip of the stem
grow clusters of tiny star-like
flowers. All species are found in dry
rocky places throughout Europe.

House mouse A mouse commonly
found wherever there are people but
not restricted to houses. It can be
found in fields, gardens and
hedgerows as well as in all kinds of
buildings. House mice are about 8.5
cm long, and feed on almost
anything.

House spider A long-legged, web-
spinning spider commonly found in
peoples' homes. As with most
spiders, the female is larger than the
male. House spiders make rather
untidy sheet webs – the familiar
'cobwebs' often seen in the corners
of rooms. There are several species,
and adults rarely live more than a
year.

Houting See WHITEFISH.

Hover-fly A large family of true flies
which can hover in mid air. They

Hover-flies

feed on pollen and nectar. Many
hover-flies look like bees and wasps
but, being true flies, have only one
pair of wings. Some of these bee-like
species lay their eggs in the nests of
bumble bees.

Humus The decayed remains of dead
organisms, mainly plants, in the soil.
It provides plants with many
essential nutrients.

Hyacinth, wild See BLUEBELL.

Hybrid The offspring of two
different species or varieties of
organisms. In the animal kingdom a
hybrid is usually infertile. An ass, for
example, is the infertile offspring of
a horse and a donkey. Many hybrid
plants on the other hand are fertile.

Hydra A tiny freshwater animal with
a tubular body (polyp) that attaches
itself to water plants. It belongs to
the same group of animals as the
corals and jellyfishes – the coelenterates. Hydras capture their prey
(small crustaceans, worms and
insect larvae) with the aid of stinging
tentacles. They can eat until they
grow to twice their normal size (a
few centimetres at most). They move
by gliding or turning somersaults,
and can reproduce either by
budding or by a sexual process.

Hydra

Hydroid See SEA FIR.

Hydrozoan Member of a group of
coelenterates that includes hydra
and the Portuguese man-of-war. As
with other coelenterates there are
two forms, polyps and medusae.
Some species have only one form or
the other but most undergo
ALTERNATION OF GENERATIONS and have
both, each at a different stage in their
life cycle. Many polyp varieties form
colonies.

Hypha Long thread-like structure of
fungi. A web of hyphae forms the
non-fruiting stage of fungi – the
mycelium.

I

Ichneumon fly

Ichneumon fly A group of long-legged, parasitic insects which are not true flies, but relatives of the bees and wasps. The female has a needle-like ovipositor at the rear of her body with which she spears an insect egg or larva and injects her own eggs. The ichneumon larva grows inside the unfortunate host, eventually killing it and eating its way out. Some ichneumon flies can locate wood-boring grubs hidden beneath the bark of trees; they use their very long ovipositors to reach them.

Imago The adult form of an insect.

Imprinting Young animals quickly learn to recognize members of their own species or family. The development of this recognition by experience is called imprinting.

Indian bean tree A deciduous tree, native to North America but grown in Europe as an ornament. It has pale, bell-shaped flowers and grows up to 20 metres high.

Inflorescence The flowering part of a plant including, along with the flower itself, the flower stalks and bracts. There may be lots of separate flowers on an inflorescence.

Shaggy ink cap

Ink cap, shaggy A grassland toadstool, easily recognized by its long, shaggy, bell-shaped cap. The gills are pink when young but turn black. The whole cap then 'melts' into an inky fluid – a process known as auto-digestion. The toadstool is often found growing on roadsides in summer and autumn and is edible before turning black.

Insect A large group of arthropods whose bodies are divided into three distinct sections – head, thorax, and abdomen – and bear three pairs of legs and a pair of feelers or antennae. Most insects also have two pairs of

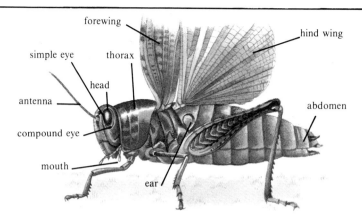

forewing

hind wing

simple eye   thorax

head

antenna

abdomen

compound eye

mouth

ear

wings. Examples include dragon-flies, grasshoppers, earwigs, bees, butterflies, and beetles.

Young insects never have fully developed wings and cannot fly. They nearly all start life as eggs, but then they follow one of two main courses of development. Some spend their early lives as NYMPHS, which often look like the adults and which gradually turn into adults. The other course of development begins with a LARVA and then passes through the PUPA or chrysalis stage before reaching maturity. Both kinds of youngsters have to change their skins several times as they grow. (See MOULTING.)

Insectivore   Member of a group of insect-eating mammals with long snouts and sharp teeth. The group includes hedgehogs, moles and shrews.

Instinct   Animal behaviour that is hereditary rather than learnt. Examples of instinctive behaviour include animal courtships, care of young and migration.

Invertebrate   Any animal without a backbone. Protozoans, crabs, worms and insects are all inverte-brates.

Iris   A group of flowering plants with sword-shaped leaves and colourful flowers. The flowers have three spreading outer petals with three smaller, almost upright inner ones. The three stigmas also look like slender petals. European irises have underground stems, or rhizomes, which often show above the ground.

Isopod   Member of a large group of crustaceans found in fresh and sea water and on land. Isopods have flat segemented bodies protected by armour-like plates, and usually seven pairs of legs, all more or less alike. In fact, the term 'isopod' means equal legs. Several kinds are parasites and most are only a few millimetres long. The woodlouse is a land-dwelling isopod.

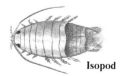

Isopod

Ivy   An evergreen, woody, climbing plant, commonly found clambering over trees, rocks and walls through-out Europe. It climbs by means of its aerial roots and produces clusters of pale green flowers.

J

Jackdaw

Jackdaw A bird belonging to the crow family. It looks similar to the carrion crow but is slightly smaller, with grey around the back of the head and blue-grey eyes. Jackdaws like to live near human habitation, where they can pick up scraps of food, nesting material and bright objects. Flocks fly in formation around their nesting sites in tree holes or cliffs, calling 'chak'.

Jay The most brightly coloured member of the crow family. It has a light pinkish-brown plumage with black on the wings and tail. Its most distinctive features are the bright

Jay

blue patches on the wings, and the white rump which is highly conspicuous when the bird is in flight. Jays imitate the calls of other birds, and even the sounds of sheep and horses. They eat the eggs of smaller birds in spring; in autumn they eat acorns, some of which they bury for future use.

Jellyfish About 200 species of marine coelenterate with transparent umbrella-shaped bodies (medusae), ringed by long hanging tentacles. Some species grow up to 2 metres across. A jellyfish's body is 90% water, and if one becomes stranded on the shore it will quickly dry out, shrinking to nothing as it evaporates. Most jellyfishes paralyse fishes and other prey by releasing poison darts from stinging cells in their tentacles. They will also sting people swimming in the sea, and some species are quite harmful.

Jellyfish

John Dory A marine fish found along the Atlantic and Mediterranean coasts. It grows up to 60 cm long and its body is flattened sideways.

Judas tree A deciduous tree, belonging to the pea family, that grows wild in the Middle East and southern Europe, and is planted elsewhere for ornamental purposes. It grows to a height of 10 metres. The deep pink flowers spring straight from the branches before the large heart-shaped leaves open.

Judas tree

Jumping spider A group of small to medium-sized spiders which leap on to their prey. They have very large eyes which help them focus clearly on their victims as they jump for the kill. About 3000 species are known.

Juniper Member of a group of coniferous trees belonging to the cypress family with fleshy, berry-like female cones. The common juniper flourishes right across Europe, Asia and North America. It grows slowly to a height of 6 metres.

Common juniper

Kelp Also known as oarweed, these large brown seaweeds have broad fronds up to 3 metres long and form dense underwater forests. They are often found along the strand line of beaches.

Kelt A salmon after it has spawned. It returns to the sea where it either dies, or remains until it is ready to spawn again.

Kestrel A bird of the falcon family noted for its hovering flight. A small falcon, with a brownish plumage and a grey head and tail, the kestrel preys mainly on mice, voles and insects. Kestrels are frequently seen

Kestrel

above roadside verges, hovering in mid air on the lookout for prey.

Kid A young goat.

Kingfisher One of Europe's most brightly coloured birds, with a glossy blue-green back and orange underparts. Kingfishers are shy birds that live by clear unpolluted streams and ponds. They dive into the water, either from a perch or in flight, to catch fish with their long sharp bills. They live in most of Europe, except the far north.

103

Kite A bird of prey, about the same size as the buzzard. It is recognized by its forked tail and soaring flight. The black kite visits Europe (but not Britain) in summer; the red kite is resident in Europe, with a few pairs living in Britain.

Kittiwake A gull which nests on rocky ledges high on sea cliffs. It is a grey-winged bird, with white head and underparts, and black legs. Kittiwakes dive to catch fish. The name comes from the sound of one of the bird's most common cries.

Black knapweed

Knapweed Several species of flowering plant related to the daisy and thistle. They have stiff hairy stems and purple-pink, thistle-like flowers. Unlike thistles, the plants are not prickly. They are common in fields and on waysides where some species may grow up to 1 metre high.

Krill Tiny shrimp-like crustaceans, from 8 to 60 mm long. Huge swarms live in the plankton near the surface of the sea, forming an important food source for fishes, birds and whales. Some krill live at depths of over 2000 metres. Many are phosphorescent, glowing at night.

L

Laburnum A deciduous tree of central and southern Europe that has been introduced further north as an ornament. It belongs to the pea family and rarely grows taller than 7 metres. It has long clusters of bright yellow flowers, and smooth brown bark. All parts of this tree are highly poisonous, especially the pods and seeds.

Laburnum

Lacewing A group of insects, with large lacy wings and long antennae. Many are bright green, while others are brown. All eat aphids. Their larvae also eat aphids and other small insects, draining the juices from their bodies.

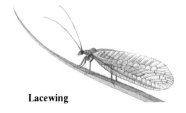

Lacewing

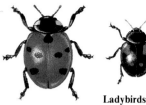

Ladybirds

Ladybird A family of beetles which feed on aphids and scale insects, and so are welcomed by gardeners. Ladybirds are rounded in shape, with short legs, and shiny wing covers. The common ladybirds are red with black spots – the number of spots varies with the species. Others are black with red spots and some are yellow and black. The bright colours warn birds that ladybirds have an unpleasant taste.

Lady's mantle Low-growing, mostly hairy plants belonging to the rose family. Lady's mantle is common to grassy places. It bears clusters of pale green, petalless flowers.

Lady's smock See CUCKOO FLOWER.

Lady's tresses Flowering plants belonging to the orchid family. The white flowers are spirally arranged in a single spike which looks like a plait of hair, giving the plants their name.

Lair A place where animals lie. The term is particularly applied to deer.

Lamina See LEAF.

Lampern See LAMPREY.

Lamprey Any of several species of primitive fish (cyclostome) with a sucking mouth and no jaws. The sea lamprey is a long eel-like fish, up to

75 cm in length. It has circular rows of horny teeth and feeds by fastening on to other fishes and sucking their blood. It enters rivers to breed. The river lamprey is similar but smaller. It is also known as the lampern.

Lampshell Also known as brachiopods, lampshells look like bivalve molluscs such as clams. They range in size from 2.5 cm to 10 cm, and are generally fastened to the sea bed by a stalk which emerges through a small hole at the end of one of the valves.

Lancelet An eel-like creature, also called amphioxus. It belongs to the chordate group, which also includes the vertebrates. Lancelets have no backbone but they have a flexible skeletal rod called a notochord and a nerve cord running down the back. The body is up to 8 cm long, pointed at both ends, and with a fin along the back. Whiskery tentacles strain food in through the mouth. Lancelets live on the sea bed, remaining buried by day with only the mouth showing. They swim by night.

Lapwing A bird also known as the green plover or peewit (from its whistling call). It has a feathered crest on its head, a metallic blue-green sheen across its back and wings, a black throat and a white belly. Lapwings flock in large numbers over ploughed fields and coastal mud-flats. They feed on insects, slugs and worms and are useful in controlling crop pests such as leatherjackets and wireworms.

Larch Member of a group of 12 coniferous trees belonging to the pine family. The leaves are borne in

River lamprey

European
larch

whorls and are shed in winter. The small upright cones have thin, almost papery scales. The European larch comes from central Europe but is planted all over the north-west, both as an ornamental tree and for its timber. It grows up to 40 metres tall. The shorter (35 metres) Japanese larch was first imported into Europe in 1861.

Larder beetle A beetle with a dark oval body, and a lighter middle section bearing dark spots. The larva of the larder beetle lives in houses, feeding on food scraps. When it develops, the adult winged insect flies off to feed on pollen from flowers.

Larder
beetle

Lark Birds noted for their sweet song and hovering flight. The lark family includes the SKYLARK, WOODLARK, and shorelark. All have small crests on their heads. They have dull brown plumages which make them difficult to spot on the ground, where they make their nests.

Larva An active stage in the development of many invertebrates, and certain vertebrates such as amphibians, which is markedly different in form from the adult. Caterpillars and tadpoles are both forms of larvae.

Latex The milky white liquid that oozes from the cut surface of certain plants. Rubber is made from the latex of the rubber tree. Dandelions also produce latex.

Laurel The name laurel is given to many kinds of ornamental bushes but the true European laurel is the sweet bay. It is a broad-leaved evergreen that can grow as high as 20 metres but is usually much shorter.

Lavender A group of usually grey-leaved, fragrant shrubs with mauve, blue or occasionally white flowers, attractive to butterflies.

Laver A dark red seaweed. In Wales, purple laver is made into a breakfast dish called laver bread.

Leaf The main food-making part of a plant. It consists of a flat green blade called the lamina and it often has a slender stalk called the petiole. The green colour is due to chlorophyll, which absorbs the energy of sunlight and uses it to power the food-making process called photosynthesis.

Leaf beetle A large group of plant-feeding beetles, many of which live in the tropics. Many are brightly coloured, often with metallic-looking wing cases. There are more than 25,000 species, including the COLORADO BEETLE which attacks potato plants. Most leaf beetles are small, under 12 mm long, and many are pests because of the damage they and their larvae do to crops.

Leaf beetles

Leaf-cutter bee A small group of solitary bees that build the cells of their nests from pieces of leaf. The female has sharp jaws and cuts neat sections from leaves, often those of roses. The leaf pieces are used to build cigar-shaped rows of brood cells, hidden inside a burrow, often in a rotting tree stump.

Leaf-cutter bee   Leafhopper

Leafhopper A group of sap-sucking bugs, some of which do considerable damage to farm crops. They are small relatives of the froghoppers, found mostly on the leaves of plants.

Leaf miner An insect which spends its early life tunnelling between the upper and lower surfaces of leaves. Most leaf miners are the grubs of small flies and moths.

Leatherjacket The larva or grub of the CRANE-FLY or daddy-long-legs. These brown leathery-looking grubs live underground and are a pest because they feed on the roots of garden plants and crops.

Leech A group of carnivorous and blood-sucking worms, found mainly in fresh water. Leeches have 34 body segments and breathe through their skins. Sucking discs at each end of their bodies enable them to cling to fishes and other animals and suck their blood. Many leeches attack small prey, including water snails.

Lek The communal mating ground of certain birds, notably many kinds of grouse. The males congregate on the lek and each takes a small area as its own private territory on which it will mate with any willing female.

Norway lemmings

Lemming A rodent closely related to the voles. It lives in colonies in the grasslands of cold northern regions where it builds underground tunnels. It does not hibernate during the winter but continues to live under the snow.

The Norway lemming is found in Scandinavia. It is a stocky animal, 14 cm long, with a short tail. About every four years the lemming population rises sharply and there is not enough food to go round. When this happens the lemmings emigrate in vast hordes. Many perish trying to cross rivers and lakes, but a few survive to set up new colonies. The wood lemming is a small relative found in coniferous forests. It too has population explosions but does not go in for mass migration.

Lepidoptera See MOTH.

Leveret A young hare.

Lichen Member of a group of very unusual plants, consisting of an intricate mixture of a fungus and an alga. The fungi in these partnerships cannot grow without their food-providing algal partners. Most lichens are extremely hardy and many grow on bare rocks in very hot or very cold places. Growth is slow and the plants are long-lived. Some form granular crusts on rocks and tree trunks; some form rosettes of more or less flat, branching lobes; others are like tiny bushes. Most are greenish-grey but some are brightly coloured. Spores come from the fungus partner only, but they cannot grow unless they find the right alga. Lichens also reproduce by scattering tiny flakes from the surface. These contain both fungus and alga.

Lily A large family of mostly herbaceous plants which includes, along with the true lilies, familiar species such as the bluebell, ramsons, meadow saffron and lily of the valley. True lilies are rarely found in NW Europe. Members of the family appear to have six-petalled flowers, but in fact the flowers have only three petals, with three petal-like sepals. Most of the plants grow from bulbs.

Lily of the valley A small, fragrant, flowering plant belonging to the lily family, though it is not a true lily. Its white, bell-shaped flowers are arranged in a loose spike, dropping down from one side of the long stem. The leaves are broad, and grow in pairs, and the fruit is a red berry. Lily of the valley is commonly found forming patches in woodland.

Lime A large family of deciduous trees, also known as lindens, and unrelated to the citrus fruit lime. Members of the family have heart-shaped leaves and produce drooping

Common lime

clusters of white or yellow flowers. The small-leaved lime grows to a height of 30 metres. Its leaves are about half the size of those of the taller large-leaved lime. The common lime is a cross between the large-leaved and small-leaved species.

Common limpets

Limpet The name of various gastropod snails with conical shells. They cling tightly to rocks on the seashore, even in stormy seas, and each limpet shell grows to fit its own piece of rock. The animals move about to graze on algae on the rocks, but always return to their own 'home base'.

Linden See LIME.

Ling (1) A marine fish belonging to the cod group, found in deep waters off the north-west coast of Europe. It is a slim fish, growing up to 2 metres long, with two dorsal fins, one of which is very long. Like many members of the cod group, the ling has a barbel on its chin. (2) See BURBOT. (3) See HEATHER.

Linnet A finch that was once a popular cage bird because of its sweet song. The male has a crimson forehead and breast during the breeding season, but the birds are otherwise dull brown. Linnets nest on open ground in gorse bushes or in hedges, and tend to roam in flocks even in the breeding season.

Linnet

Litter (1) The collective name for a group of babies born at one time. Mammals such as pigs and cats have litters. (2) The layer of dead leaves on a woodland floor.

Little owl The little owl does most of its hunting at dawn or dusk, and is often seen and heard by day. Its cry is shrill and plaintive. Little owls like open country, but often nest under eaves. Favourite perches include telegraph poles and tall fences.

Liver fluke See FLUKE.

Liverwort Green flowerless plants closely related to the mosses. There are two types: leafy liverworts that look very similar to mosses; and flat liverworts that look more like green seaweed. The life story of liverworts is similar to that of mosses, with both a sexual reproductive stage and a spore producing stage. The spore capsules are round and black, and they split open to form a star shape when they release their spores.

Lizard A reptile with, usually, four legs and a long tail. Some species, such as the SLOW WORM, have no legs at all and look like snakes. Most lizards feed on insects and other small creatures, though some eat vegetable matter as well. Several species have a strange defence against attack: they can shed their tails which continue to wriggle and distract the enemy while the lizards escape. A new, shorter tail grows in due course. See GREEN LIZARD, SAND LIZARD, VIVIPAROUS LIZARD and WALL LIZARD.

Common wall lizard

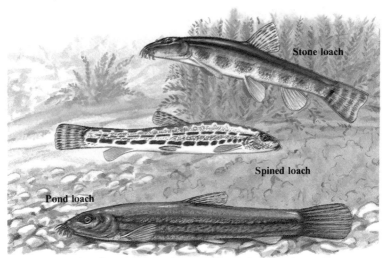

Stone loach

Spined loach

Pond loach

Loach A family of over 200 species of small, slender fish, three of which are found in Europe. Loaches have barbels around their mouths. They live on the bottom of ponds or rivers, eating insect larvae and other small animals.

Lobster, common A large crustacean which lives on the sea bed. Lobsters have long antennae. eyes on stalks and five pairs of legs. The first pair form large pincers, or claws. Besides walking, lobsters can also move by swimming backwards. They are mainly active at night, feeding on living and dead animal matter and bits of seaweed. Their colour varies from blue to dark green.

Locust A group of insects related to the grasshoppers, some of which very occasionally visit NW Europe. There are many species of locust, some of which cause terrible damage to crops in Africa by swarming in vast numbers.

Locust tree A spiny, deciduous tree belonging to the pea family and also called the false acacia. A native of North America, it was first brought to Europe in the 1600s. It is often grown in parks and gardens, where it reaches a height of 30 metres. Its white, pea-like flowers grow in long clusters.

Long-eared bat, common A small bat, 4.5 cm long, found over most of Europe. Its ears are almost as long as its body. The bats eat mainly moths, often plucking them from leaves.

Long-eared bat

Long-eared owl An owl with long ear tufts which are not ears but feathers. It lives mostly among coniferous trees, making its home in the old nests of squirrels or large birds. It feeds on insects, small mammals such as voles, and even young birds.

Longhorn beetle

Longhorn beetle   A large group of beetles with very long antennae. The largest beetles are 15 cm long. Some species are disguised to resemble wasps or pieces of vegetation. Many cause great damage to trees, for the larvae spend two years or more as wood-boring grubs.

Long-tailed field mouse   See WOOD MOUSE.

Long-tailed tit   A tiny bird that belongs to a different group from the other tits. Unlike them, it has a pinkish colouring and a long tail, and builds its nest in the open instead of in a hole. In winter long-tailed tits form large groups, and roost huddled together for warmth.

Loon   See DIVER.

Loosestrife   Two unrelated groups of flowering plants are given the name loosestrife. The yellow and tufted loosestrife are both yellow-flowered members of the primrose family. Their flowers are arranged in clusters. The purple loosestrife belongs to a separate, small family. It has purple-pink flowers arranged in whorled spikes. Both groups are found in damp places and by fresh water.

Lords and ladies   A strange flowering plant which is also known as cuckoo-pint, Adam and Eve and parson-in-the-pulpit. It has a large, yellow-green hood enveloping a thick, foul-smelling spike. The tiny, green, single-sexed flowers are arranged around the base of the spike. Insects attracted by the smell soon become trapped inside the base of the hood, where they pollinate the flowers. When they escape they go on to pollinate other flowers. The plant has arrow-shaped leaves and produces highly poisonous, bright red berries. It is commonly found in woodlands and hedgerows.

Louse   A group of wingless insects that are parasites of birds and mammals, including humans. Lice are flat and hairy, with strong claws for clinging to the fur or feathers of their host. Sucking lice feed on the blood of mammals; biting lice live mainly on birds, chewing the skin and feathers. The eggs, or nits, are laid on feathers, hair and clothing. Lice cause itching of the skin and carry disease.

Human louse

Lugworm   Bristle worms that burrow deep into the sand or mud of the sea bed or shore. Their segmented bodies grow up to 30 cm long, and the worms are popular with fishermen as bait. They feed on dead remains which they extract from the sand and mud they swallow. The coiled casts found on sandy or muddy beaches at low tide are made by lugworms.

Lumpsucker   A bottom-living marine fish found all around the north and west coasts of Europe. It has two of its fins fused together to form a sucker under its body.

M

Mackerel A shoaling fish that spends winter in deep water close to the sea bottom. It spends the spring and summer in coastal waters feeding on a variety of fishes. It is usually about 40 cm long, with wavy blue stripes running down its back and a series of small fins in front of its tail.

Madder, wild A clambering, ever-green, flowering plant related to the bedstraws. Its stem is weak and, together with the leaves, is covered in prickles. The pale yellow-green flowers are arranged in stalked clusters. The plant produces small black berries and is commonly found in woods and scrubland.

Maggot The grub of certain types of flies. It has no legs and its head is minute.

Magnolia A tree or shrub widely cultivated for its beautiful, sweet-smelling flowers. There are several species, some of which are evergreen.

Magpie A black and white member of the crow family, with a long tail. Much of the black plumage, closely viewed, shows a green or dark blue sheen. Magpies are usually seen in pairs, hunting for food together. The birds eat eggs and young chicks. Like jackdaws, they like to collect bright objects.

Magpie

Magpie moth

Magpie moth Named for its black and white pattern, which also includes brownish-yellow markings, the magpie moth is usually seen in gardens and around hedgerows.

Maidenhair See GINKGO.

Mallard A wild duck, common on marshes, coastal mud-flats and lakes. Mallard are often seen on ornamental ponds. The female bird is speckled brown; the male has grey and reddish-brown feathers, with a handsome dark green head. Mallard feed on water animals, insects, seeds and berries. They nest on the ground.

Mallow A group of hairy flowering plants with mostly pink, five-petalled flowers arranged in whorls at the base of the leaves. The leaves are usually rounded and lobed, and the flowers are sometimes cup-shaped, as in the case of the woody tree mallow. Most species are found on waste ground.

Mammal Any of the large class of backboned animals in which the female feeds her young with milk from her own body. All mammals have warm blood, and with a few exceptions they are clothed with hair. Apart from egg-laying mono-tremes such as the duck-billed platypus, they all give birth to active young. Badgers, cats, mice, whales, and humans are all mammals.

Mandarin A duck which, as the name suggests, comes from China but is now found in parks and water gardens all over the world. The male is brightly coloured, with distinctive orange tufts on his cheeks.

Mandible (1) The lower jaw of any backboned animal. (2) Part of the feeding apparatus of an insect or a crustacean.

Mange A skin disease of mammals, including humans, caused by the presence of certain mites. These tiny creatures damage the skin cells and cause intense itching.

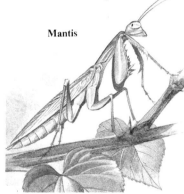

Mantis

Mantis A group of insects, also known as praying mantises because they often stay motionless in a prayer-like attitude while waiting for prey to come along. Mantises have long spiny front legs which they can shoot out at great speed to seize any insect in reach. They are related to cockroaches and live mostly in the tropics, though one species, the common mantis of Europe, reaches as far north as Paris and southern Belgium.

Mantle The soft 'cloak' of rather thick skin covering the bodies of mulluscs. It is largely hidden inside the shells of snails and bivalves, but it can be seen draped over the backs of slugs.

Maple A family of 150 species of deciduous trees, of which four are native to Europe: several others have been imported as ornamental trees. Maples have small, greenish-yellow flowers and paired, winged fruits that are scattered by the wind. The leaves are palmate (hand shaped) and usually deeply lobed. The field maple is a small tree, up to 20 metres tall, frequently found growing in hedgerows. The Norway maple grows very rapidly to a height of 30 metres. It produces its bright

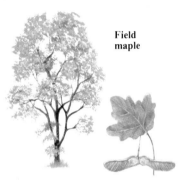

Field maple

yellow flowers before it comes into leaf. The ash-leaved maple is a native of eastern North America, but is widely used ornamentally in towns in Europe because it grows quickly and apparently tolerates pollution. It is also known as the box elder and it grows up to 20 metres.

Mare's-tail A waterweed often found completely submerged in ponds or streams. It is unbranched and upright, and its thin, dark green leaves are arranged in whorls.

Marjoram A fragrant, flowering plant related to the dead-nettle. Marjoram has stalked oval leaves and purple flowers arranged in loose clusters. It is widely cultivated; the leaves are used for flavouring food.

Marmot, Alpine The only European ground squirrel, living mainly in the

Alpine marmots

Alps and Pyrenees but introduced to some other mountain areas. This rodent is larger than the tree squirrels, up to 55 cm long. Marmots live in colonies above the tree-line on sunny slopes, where they feed on grasses and other plants. They dig burrows and hibernate during the winter.

Marram grass A grass found mostly on sand dunes, where it stabilizes the dunes by binding the sand with its network of rhizomes (underground stems). The grass has long, slender, sharply-pointed leaves and oval flowering heads.

Marsh frog A large green frog that lives mostly in south-western Europe and from Germany eastwards, but which has been introduced to Romney Marsh in England. Up to 15 cm long, it is the largest European frog. It is very noisy and spends more of its time in the water than most frogs.

Marsh tit A small black-headed tit, very similar in habit and appearance to the willow tit. Both birds live in woodlands and make their nests in holes in trees. Unlike other tits, they do not go around in flocks.

Marten A carnivore, similar in shape to its cousin the stoat, only larger – about the size of a cat. There are two very similar species found in

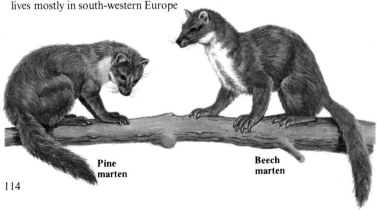

Pine marten

Beech marten

Europe. Both are mainly nocturnal and have bushy tails, short legs and dark brown fur. The claws are strongly curved and sharp.

Martin Migratory birds similar to swallows but with far shorter forked tails. They fly north for the summer from South Africa and can usually be seen high in the sky catching insects on the wing. The two most common European species are the house and the sand martin. House martins build their nests of mud on the outside of buildings, often under the eaves. Sand martins build their nests in holes in sand banks.

House martin

Mason wasp A group of solitary wasps that usually build nests of sand and saliva, often in holes in walls. Some species build a hollow tower around the entrance to the nest. The nest consists of a number of brood cells in which the female lays her eggs. The young are left to grow up without the aid of workers.

Mat grass A plant belonging to the large grass family. It is a low, slender-stemmed grass which creeps over the ground.

May See HAWTHORN.

Maybug See COCKCHAFER.

Mayfly A group of insects, related to the dragonflies, which live near water. Mayflies have long slender bodies, delicate wings and long trailing tails. The young, called nymphs, spend their lives in the water. The adults have very short lives, rarely more than a week and only a few hours in some species.

Mayweed Several species of flowering plant belonging to the daisy family. The scentless mayweed has a branched stem with daisy-like flowers and finely segmented, hair-like leaves. The pineapple mayweed smells of pineapple.

Meadow grass The name given to a group of our commonest and most widespread grasses.

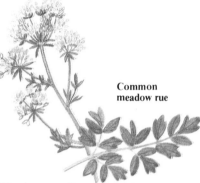

Common meadow rue

Meadow rue Several flowering plants of the buttercup family. All species are characterized by their clusters of delicate, four-petalled flowers. The flowers are unusual in that the actual petals are rather inconspicuous, but the stamens are long and prominent, and give the flowers their colour and feathery appearance.

Meadow saffron A small flowering plant of the lily family that prefers damp soil. It has solitary, crocus-like flowers in shades of pinkish-purple, and the large, bright green leaves die before the flowers appear. The plants flower in autumn and produce an almost oval fruit in spring. They grow in woods and meadows.

Meadowsweet

Meadowsweet A tall flowering plant of the rose family, often found on the banks of streams and ditches. It has a delicate scent and dense clusters of creamy, feathery flowers. The plant grows up to 1 metre tall.

Medick Mostly low-growing, flowering plants belonging to the pea family. They have trefoil leaves and yellow, clover-like flowers.

Medlar A small deciduous tree belonging to the rose family. It has long dull leaves with hardly any stalks. The white flowers have five narrow sepals projecting beyond the petals, and produce small sour fruits, used for making jelly.

Medusa The free-swimming, saucer-shaped stage in the life cycle of many coelenterates. Jelly-fishes are medusae.

Melanin A pigment responsible for the brown colours of many animals. There are actually two main kinds of melanin – a very dark brown one and a yellowish one.

Merganser Ducks which live by the sea most of the year but often breed on freshwater lakes. The most common merganser is the red-breasted. Both male and female birds have head crests. The merganser's bill is saw-toothed for catching fish under water; the bird dives from the surface to catch its prey.

Merlin A bird of prey and the smallest European falcon. The male is grey-blue, the female browner. Merlins are found on open moorland, flying swiftly to catch small birds and insects. The nest is a hollow on the ground or on a rock ledge.

Mermaid's purse The horny egg-case of skates and dogfishes. It is more or less rectangular, with a string at each corner. The strings become wrapped round seaweeds to anchor the case. Empty cases, usually without their strings, are often washed up on the seashore.

Metamorphosis A total change of form during the life of an animal. Good examples can be found among frogs and toads, which start life as legless tadpoles; and also among insects – the butterfly grows from a caterpillar, and the house-fly from a wriggling maggot.

Micro-organism Any microscopically small plant or animal, such as a bacterium or a protozoan.

Midge Small mosquito-like flies often seen in swarms on warm summer evenings. Biting midges feed by sucking blood, but the non-biting and gall midges are harmless to other animals. Many midges lay their eggs in water. The aquatic larvae of some non-biting midges are called bloodworms.

Midwife toad This animal is so named because the male wraps the strings of eggs around his hind legs, and carries them until they are ready to hatch into tadpoles. Midwife toads hunt at night, hiding by day in piles of stones or crevices in walls.

Midwife toads

Mignonette, wild   A flowering plant commonly found on bare or disturbed ground. It bears small, yellowish-green flowers arranged in a spike, and produces erect, oblong pods.

Migration   The regular movement of animals from one area to another and back again, usually on a seasonal basis.

Mildew   A group of parasitic fungi that form on the leaves of higher plants. The term is also more widely used to describe any fungal growth that covers a surface with fine threads or hyphae.

Milk cap   One of a group of toadstools that exude milky droplets when the gills are broken.

Milkweed butterfly   See MONARCH.

Milkwort   A group of flowering plants. The common milkwort has pointed leaves and blue, bell-shaped flowers; it grows best on chalky soils. The shrubby milkwort, a mountain species, is a low evergreen shrub with pink, purple, yellow or white flowers.

Miller's thumb   See BULLHEAD.

Millipede   A group of many-legged arthropods that move about slowly in soil and dead leaves, feeding on decaying vegetation. Most species are long and slender, and almost every segment of their bodies bears two pairs of legs. For defence, millipedes give off an unpleasant fluid.

Mimicry   Some harmless creatures resemble poisonous or otherwise unpleasant ones that are protected by WARNING COLORATION. This is called mimicry, and it enables the harmless creature also to escape many of its enemies. Some of the best examples of mimicry are found among insects.

Mimosa   An evergreen tree, native to Australia, but widely grown in Europe as an ornament, especially for its yellow flower clusters. It belongs to the pea family.

Mining bee

Mining bee   A group of solitary bees which dig burrows up to 20 cm deep, usually in sandy soil, in which to build their nests. Like other solitary bees, the female mining bee provides each egg with a food supply of honey and pollen before sealing the brood cell. She takes no further interest in the young, which develop underground and emerge the following spring as adults.

European
mink

Mink A nocturnal carnivore that looks like its smaller relative, the weasel. Its dark brown fur is highly prized. The European mink is about 38 cm long with a long body and tail and short legs, and it has a little white mark on its upper and lower lip. It is found mostly in France. The larger American mink has escaped from fur farms and is found in Scandinavia and the British Isles. It has white only on the lower lip. Mink live near water and are excellent swimmers.

Minnow One of the smallest fishes of the carp family – a full-grown minnow is only 4 to 9 cm long. It lives in clear rivers and sometimes in brackish water. Minnows form an important part of the diet of larger fishes such as pike.

Minotaur beetle A scarab beetle, also called the horned dung beetle. The male bears bull-like horns on its thorax, from which it gets its name (the Minotaur in Greek mythology was a horned creature – half man, half bull). The minotaur beetle lives in a burrow close to rabbit warrens; it feeds on rabbit dung, collecting the

Minotaur
beetle

droppings and filling its burrow with them as food for its young.

Mint A number of sweet-smelling plants belonging to the same family as the dead-nettles. Mints have square stems and dense whorls or spikes of small purple flowers. The broad leaves are the most fragrant part of the plant and are used to flavour food.

Mistletoe A semi-parasitic woody plant that grows on the branches of trees, especially on apples and poplars. Mistletoe does not have any roots, but sends out suckers which draw water and mineral salts from the branches. It has pairs of tough yellowish leaves and inconspicuous green flowers. The mistletoe produces sticky white berries in winter, and is widely used as a Christmas decoration.

Mite A tiny spider-like arachnid. Some mites live as parasites inside other animals, or on their skins. Others feed on rotting plant matter or prey on other small invertebrate animals. Most mites have four pairs of legs. They are found almost everywhere: on land, in fresh water and even in hot springs.

Mole A small insectivore that spends most of its time underground. It is a tube-shaped creature about 14 cm long, with large spade-like front feet that are ideally suited to digging. The mole lives in a maze of underground tunnels and feeds mainly on earthworms and other small creatures. Its eyesight is very poor and it relies mainly on smell and hearing.

Mollusc Any member of the large phylum of animals that includes the slugs and snails (see GASTROPOD), the BIVALVES, and the squids and octopuses (see CEPHALOPOD). The name simply means 'soft' and refers to the animals' soft bodies, although many are actually protected by a hard shell. Some mollusc shells bear the shiny inner lining known as mother-of-pearl. The phylum is the second largest in the animal kingdom, with about 90,000 species. Only the arthropods have more species than the molluscs.

Money spider A small spider that is abundant in grasslands and often found indoors. It is so light that it floats through the air hanging to a silken thread spun by its spinnerets (silk organs).

Monkey flower

Monkey flower A flowering, waterside plant related to the foxglove. The monkey flower was introduced into Europe from Alaska in 1812 and has since spread to many riverbanks. It is a low, creeping plant, easily recognized by its bright yellow, two-lipped flowers which are dotted with red spots.

Monkey puzzle An evergreen coniferous tree, also called the Chile pine. It gets its popular name of monkey puzzle because it looks too difficult for even a monkey to climb. The horizontal branches have turned-up ends, and bear broad leathery needles with spiny tips.

Monkfish A small bottom-living shark, about 1.2 metres long. It has a broad body that makes it look similar to a ray, and lives in deep water, moving to shallow coastal waters in the summer.

Monkshood A tall poisonous plant of the buttercup family. Monkshood grows up to 90 cm tall and gets its name from its flowers which resemble a monk's cowl. The leaves are palmately lobed and the bright purple flowers are arranged in a long spike. The plant is found in damp woodlands and by streams.

Moor frog

Moor frog A close relative of the common frog, sometimes known as the field frog. It is a small brownish frog, about 8 cm long. Some males turn blue in the breeding season. Moor frogs are found in very damp places. They do not live in Britain.

Moorhen A water bird similar to the coot, but slightly smaller and with a red patch at the base of its red bill. It swims with a head-jerking motion, and on land constantly jerks its tail. Moorhens feed on insects, worms and water plants and animals. They live on rivers, lakes and park ponds.

Moose See ELK.

Morel Member of a group of edible mushrooms with distinctive crinkled caps. The common morel is found in grasslands and light woodlands.

Mosquito A group of true flies that are renowned for biting humans. In fact not all mosquitoes bite people; only certain species suck the blood of mammals and even then only the females are blood-suckers. They pierce the skin with their long proboscises.

Lepidoptera, which means 'scale-wing'. Their wings are covered with tiny scales which give them their colour. Most moths fly at night and many fold their wings flat into a 'delta-wing' shape when at rest, unlike butterflies which usually rest with wings folded together above their bodies. Moths often have feather-like antennae and, unlike butterflies, their antennae very rarely have knobs on the end. This provides a good way of telling the two insects apart. Moths feed mainly on nectar from flowers, and their larvae are called caterpillars. Like butterflies, they have a four-stage life cycle, from egg to larva, pupa and finally adult form.

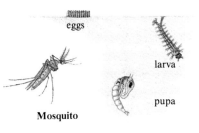

Mosquito

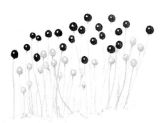

Pin mould

Moss A group of green flowerless plants closely related to the liver-worts. Mosses grow in damp places forming soft mats or cushions on the ground. They have short slender stems with thin leaves. There are no proper roots but short hairs anchor the plants to the ground. At certain times of the year male and female sexual organs develop. Fertilization results in the formation of green capsules on the ends of long stalks. These produce the spores which scatter and eventually grow into new plants.

Moss animal See SEA MAT.

Moth Along with butterflies, moths form a large insect group, the

Mould (1) Any of the many relatively simple fungi that spread all over the materials on which they grow and cover them with fluffy or spongy coats. Penicillium is a bluish-green mould that grows on many stale foods, including cakes and bread. Pin moulds are fluffy white moulds, also found on our foods, that produce their spores in tiny black 'pin heads'. (2) A rich soil, especially one full of HUMUS.

Moulting The changing or renewal of the plumage or other covering of an animal. Mammals usually moult twice a year. Birds also change their feathers regularly, usually just after the breeding season. Insects and other arthropods change their complete skins several times as they grow up. Their hard outer coats do not grow with the animal. When the skin gets tight, the animal bursts out of it to expose a new skin that has already formed underneath.

Mouse A small rodent closely related to the rats. It looks similar to a vole but has a longer snout and tail, and larger ears. The tail is almost naked. Most species of mouse live in the wild and are rarely seen but the

Mullein A group of mostly tall flowering plants of the figwort family. Mulleins have flat, five-petalled flowers usually arranged in a bulky spike. Some species are downy. The great mullein is one of the most common species. It is covered in thick, white, woolly hairs and has yellow flowers. It is a plant of waysides and wasteland and is often known as Aaron's rod.

House mouse

Northern birch mice

HOUSE MOUSE lives in close association with humans. See also HARVEST MOUSE and WOOD MOUSE.

Mouse-eared bat, greater One of the largest bats in Europe, 7.5 cm long with a wingspan of 45 cm. In summer the bats spend the daytime in the lofts of houses, moving to cellars or caves for the winter.

Mulberry A group of deciduous trees with broad, often heart-shaped leaves. The black mulberry comes from Asia, and is grown for its blackberry-like fruit. It reaches a height of 12 metres. Much rarer is the white mulberry which has white or pink fruit. Silkworms feed on its leaves.

Mullet A name given to two un-related groups of fishes, the grey mullets and the red mullets. Several species of grey mullet can be found in European coastal waters. They grow to around 50 cm long and feed on plankton. The smaller red mullets, though more common in the Atlantic and Mediterranean, are occasionally found in the North Sea and English Channel.

Muntjac A small deer from eastern China. It is little larger than a fox and is the smallest deer in Europe. The males have tiny curved antlers. Muntjacs hide in woodlands.

Mushroom A term used for a small group of edible toadstools.

Muskrat   A large North American vole, about 35 cm long, valued for its fur (musquash). It was introduced into Europe in 1905 and has since escaped from fur farms. It is not found in Britain. Muskrats are twice the size of water voles and are even better swimmers. They burrow in river banks and sometimes make nests similar to beaver lodges. They feed mainly on water plants.

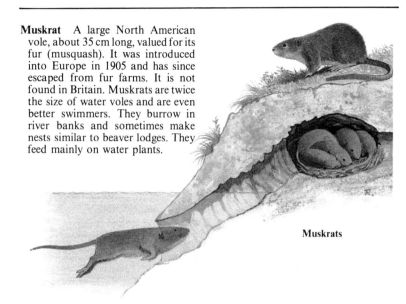

Muskrats

Mussel   A group of bivalve molluscs found both in fresh and salt water. Marine mussels are most often found on rocky shores and in river estuaries. They cling to rocks by thin threads, known as the beard or byssus, and open their shells to feed.

Common mussel

Bearded horse mussel

Mustard   A number of plants in the cabbage family. Mustard plants are grown for their hot seeds, used as a spice; the seedlings are also eaten in salad. The flowers are yellow and the leaves are tough with ragged edges.

Mycelium   The mass of slender threads making up a mould or other fungus. It soaks up food from the material on which it grows. The mycelium of a toadstool is usually under the ground or hidden in dead wood.

Myrobalan   See CHERRY PLUM.

Myrtle   A number of evergreen shrubs or trees. The common myrtle has white or pink flowers and blue-black berries. (The bog myrtle is a member of the willow family.)

Myxomatosis   A disease of rabbits which very nearly eradicated the animals from Britain and other parts of Europe in the 1950s. It is caused by a virus which is carried by blood-sucking fleas and mosquitoes.

N

Natterer's bat

Natterer's bat A small bat, only 4.5 cm long, found in most of Europe except the far north. It forms huge colonies, usually in trees near water but often in buildings.

Natterjack toad This toad does not hop like other toads and frogs, but runs like a mouse. It is about 8 cm long and is found in western Europe, including the British Isles. Natterjacks can easily be distinguished from other toads by the bright yellow strip running down the centre of the back. They have harsh, noisy voices and often sing in a chorus which can be heard a long way off.

Natterjack toad

Natural selection The driving force behind EVOLUTION. Any individual born with an advantage over other members of its species (i.e. a characteristic which increases its chances of survival) is more likely to live to produce young. If the characteristic is hereditary, the number of individuals possessing it will gradually increase while those individuals without it will eventually die out. This process of selection is often called 'survival of the fittest'.

Nectar The sugary liquid produced by many flowers that attracts bees and other insects. While drinking the nectar, the insects unknowingly pollinate the flowers so that they can set seed.

Nectary See FLOWER.

Nekton The collective name for all the free-swimming animals in the sea or in a lake. They can control their own movements and are not just carried by the currents like plankton.

Nematode Any of the huge group of animals commonly known as roundworms. Most are very small and their bodies are not made up of rings or segments like the earthworms. Millions live in the soil and in fresh and salt water, feeding on decaying matter. Others attack plant roots. Some of the larger ones live as parasites inside other animals, including man.

Nettle A group of flowering plants noted for the stinging hairs on their stems and leaves. These hairs protect the nettle from hungry animals. The common nettle grows in gardens and hedgerows; it has clusters of small green flowers. The plants called DEAD-NETTLES, though similar in appearance, belong to a different plant group.

Newt A small lizard-like amphibian closely related to the salamanders. Unlike lizards, newts have no scales and are easily distinguished by their flattened (rather than rounded) tails. They live in or close to water, and all species lay their eggs in water. As with frogs and toads, the eggs hatch into tiny larvae called tadpoles that gradually develop into the adult forms. The CRESTED NEWT, PALMATE NEWT and SMOOTH NEWT are three common European species.

Nightingale A bird belonging to the thrush family. It is rather dull to look at, a little smaller than a song thrush, but it is considered to be one of the finest singers of all birds. It gets its name from its habit of singing at night, but it also sings by day. The birds migrate from Africa in the spring to breed in Europe.

Nightjar A bird, also called the goatsucker, which visits Europe in summer. It flies at night in search of insects, catching them in its gaping mouth. Its night cry is a continual 'chirring' sound. The nightjar lives on heathland and light woodland, and nests on the ground.

Nightshade Poisonous flowering plants, related to henbane and thorn-apple. Deadly nightshade has pointed oval leaves, purple-green flowers and black berries. It likes a lime soil. Bittersweet, or woody nightshade, has star-shaped purple flowers and berries which turn from green to red. Nightshades usually grow in woods or damp places.

Woody nightshade

Noctule bat

Noctule bat One of the largest European bats, about 7.5 cm long, and easily recognizable by its size and rich brown colour.

Node A joint or junction on a plant stem. It is often swollen, especially in grasses, and one or more leaves or roots may spring from it.

Notochord A flexible rod, replaced by a backbone in most adult chordates.

Nut A fruit with a woody coat and normally containing just a single seed.

Nutcracker A bird belonging to the crow family. It is brown with white spots, and behaves rather like the jay. Its food, however, is vegetarian; the nutcracker's usual diet is pine seeds. It lives in pine forests from Europe to eastern Asia.

Nuthatch An agile tree bird that can run down as well as up tree trunks in its search for insects. It also wedges nuts in cracks in the bark and hammers them open. Nuthatches have short tails, blue-grey backs and a black streak running through the eye. They nest in holes in trees, reducing the entrance hole to their own size with mud.

Nymph The young of any insect that grows up gradually without any chrysalis stage. The nymph looks quite like the adult but its wings are not fully developed. Dragonflies and grasshoppers are among the insects that have nymphs.

O

Oak A group of 800 or so species of broad-leaved tree, belonging to the beech family, of which only half a dozen are commonly grown in Europe. All oaks produce acorns as fruit, traditionally used to feed pigs. The best-known oaks are the common, pedunculate or English oak, and the similar sessile or durmast oak, both with deeply-lobed leaves that fall in the autumn. Both are big trees, reaching heights of 40 metres, and living for hundreds of years. The acorns of the common oak are borne on long stalks, while those of the sessile (stalkless) oak grow close to their twigs. The holm oak is an evergreen with deep green, leathery leaves.

Oak-apple See GALL.

Oarweed See KELP.

Octopus Marine molluscs belonging to the cephalopod group and related to the squids and cuttlefish. An octopus has eight tentacles, armed with suckers with which it seizes prey such as crabs. It has a bag-like body, large eyes, and a beaked mouth, and moves rapidly by shooting out a jet of water from a siphon tube. Octopuses can change colour to blend with their surroundings, and give off an inky 'smoke-screen' to confuse an enemy. The common octopus of European coasts grows up to 3 metres across the tentacles, but it is usually very much smaller.

Olive A family of trees and shrubs including the ash, jasmine, privet, lilac and olive.

Omnivore Any animal that regularly eats a mixture of plant and animal material in its diet. Humans and badgers are both examples of omnivores.

Operculum (1) The flap covering the gills of most fishes. (2) The horny disc with which many snails close their shells.

Orache Flowering plants related to the goosefoot. Unlike the goosefoot, however, the oraches have separate male and female flowers. They are often found on rough ground, close to the sea. Varieties include the common, grass-leaved, spear-leaved and frosted oraches.

Orange-tip

Orange-tip Only the male orange-tip butterfly has the orange blotches on its wing tips which give this insect its name. The female is plain white above. Both sexes have green mottling underneath. These butter-flies feed on flowers, often on uncut roadside verges and meadows. The orange-tip caterpillar is bright green and feeds on cuckoo flower and related plants.

Orchid A large family of over 20,000 species of flowering plant, most of which grow in the tropics, often

Bee orchid

living on other plants. Those living in cooler climates mostly root into the soil. The roots often thicken to form tubers. The flowers vary greatly in shape from species to species, but they are all two-lipped and frequently spurred. Many orchids are named after animals which their blooms resemble, for instance the bee, fly, and man orchids. Other orchids include LADY'S TRESSES and TWAYBLADES. Orchids are grown commercially for their flowers. Many wild species in Europe are becoming rare.

Order Each class of plants or animals is divided into orders. For example, the class of mammals includes the orders of carnivores, primates, and rodents. Each order in turn contains one or more families. See also CLASSIFICATION.

Organism Any living creature, plant or animal.

Oriole See GOLDEN ORIOLE.

Ormer A gastropod mollusc, related to the limpets and also called the ear shell, or abalone. Its shell is roughly ear-shaped and has a line of holes, like portholes, through which the animal lets out water after passing it over the gills. Ormers feed on seaweed and debris.

Ormer

Osier A deciduous tree belonging to the willow family which grows to a height of 10 metres. It has long, pliable shoots called withies which are used for basket-making. The leaves are long and narrow and, as with all willows, the male and female flowers are arranged in catkins.

Osprey A bird of prey which hunts fish and is also known as the fish hawk. It is mostly brown, with white mottled underparts. The osprey dives into the water to catch its prey, seizing the fish in its talons and carrying it off. It nests in trees. It is extremely rare in Britain with only a few well-protected pairs nesting in the Scottish Highlands.

Otter A carnivore belonging to the weasel family. It is about 75 cm long with a long body and tail and short legs. The feet are webbed and the fur is shiny and dark brown. Otters live on the banks of rivers and lakes, and also by the sea. They hunt at night,

Otter

feeding on fish and other water animals. They are found all over Europe but are becoming rare.

Ovary (1) That part of a female animal where the eggs or ova are produced. (2) That part of the carpel of a flower which contains the ovules. After fertilization, the ovules become seeds and the ovary forms all or part of the fruit.

Ovipositor The egg-laying equipment of female insects. It is often hidden inside the body, but in some insects it is like a sword or a spear sticking out from the hind end. These insects push their eggs into crevices or even into other animals. The ovipositor in bees, wasps and ants has been converted into a sting, but only female insects can have such a weapon.

Owl Birds of prey that are more often heard than seen. Owls are renowned for their mournful cries at night. Their flight is silent, the sound of their wings muffled by their fluffy feathers. Owls have flattened, disc-shaped faces with sharply hooked bills. They fly mostly at night, feeding on small animals which they seize in their grasping feet. They have large forward-facing eyes and can see well in the dark. There are over 130 species worldwide of which about 10 are found in Europe. They include the BARN OWL, LITTLE OWL, LONG-EARED OWL, TAWNY OWL and SCOPS OWL.

Oxlip A flowering plant related to the primrose and cowslip, with which it may cross-breed. It is a low-growing plant, with hairy leaves and nodding yellow flowers, often found in large numbers in meadows and woods. The so-called false oxlip is a cross between a primrose and a cowslip.

Ox-tongue Flowering plants of the hawkweed group, similar to the dandelion in that the leaves are oval

Bristly ox-tongue

and ragged, and the flowers are yellow-orange. Ox-tongues grow in grassland and waste ground. One variety, the bristly ox-tongue, is covered with hairs.

Oyster A group of bivalve molluscs found on shallow muddy shores. The lower valve is thick and curved; the upper valve, which is thinner and flatter, is opened by a strong muscle. When closed, the oyster's shells are hard to pull apart. Oysters lay many millions of eggs which hatch into swimming larvae. When adult, the oyster 'cements' its lower valve to the sea bed. If grit enters the shell, it protects its soft body by encasing the grit in a pearl.

Oystercatcher A bird of the sea-shore, related to the plovers. It has handsome black and white plumage and a long, bright orange bill. Its diet includes shellfish (not often oysters), shrimps, worms and other seashore animals and it is usually seen picking its way along the water's edge, searching for food.

Oyster drill A sea snail that preys on other molluscs, such as oysters, by drilling into their shells and sucking out their soft flesh.

Oyster fungus A bracket fungus that, unlike many other bracket fungi, has gills under the cap. It grows in tiers on trunks and dead stumps of deciduous trees, especially beech.

Oyster plant See SALSIFY.

P

Painted lady

Painted lady   A colourful butterfly that spends the winter in Africa and southern Europe and migrates northwards in late spring. It is a strong flier but, like the red admiral, it cannot live through the cold of a northern winter. The caterpillars feed on thistles.

Palmate leaf   A leaf which is divided into lobes or leaflets like the fingers of a hand.

Palmate newt   So called because the males have palmate (webbed) rear feet in the breeding season. It is the smallest newt in Europe, only 9 cm long including the tail. It breeds in a variety of ponds and lakes, including salty pools on the coast.

Palmate newt

Palp   A type of sensory limb found on the heads of insects and various other animals, especially around the mouth. They are often used for smelling and tasting food.

Pansy   Flowering plants similar to their close relatives, the violets, but with larger, flatter flowers. The wild pansy has yellow or violet flowers, and grows in open ground, sometimes on sand dunes.

Wild pansy

Paper wasp   A relatively slender social wasp that builds a small paper nest from chewed-up wood, containing just one layer of cells. The nest looks rather like a small umbrella, and is generally found attached to plants or buildings. The insect is common in southern Europe but does not live in Britain.

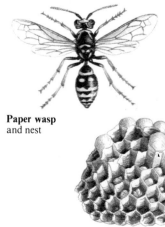

Paper wasp and nest

Paramecium This tiny oblong creature is the commonest pond ciliate. It reproduces sexually and by division.

Parasite A plant or animal that lives on or in another species and takes food from it without giving anything in return.

Parasol mushroom A grassland toadstool, easily recognized by its scaly cap with a central nipple and by the wavy pattern on the stalk. The mushroom often grows near trees and is very good to eat. The shaggy parasol is similar but has no nipple and no wavy markings on the stalk. Parasol mushrooms often form fairy rings.

Parsons-in-the-pulpit See LORDS AND LADIES.

Partridge A game bird that looks rather like a plump, short-legged pigeon. The English, grey or common partridge lives on cultivated land, heaths, moors and sand dunes. It is frequently reared on estates for shooting. Another European partridge is the larger red-legged or French partridge.

Pasque flower A short, flowering plant closely related to the anemone. It has finely divided, feathery leaves which, along with the stem, are covered with fine hairs. Its large flowers are petalless but have vivid, usually purple, petal-like sepals.

Passeriformes See PERCHING BIRD.

Pea A group of flowering plants which includes the edible garden pea and blackeyed pea or cowpea, as well as the sweet pea (cultivated only for its flowers) and the wild spring pea and sea pea. They are climbing plants which scramble over hedges and undershrubs by means of their long tendrils. Peas belong to a large family of plants which also includes the vetches, clovers, gorse and laburnum. All bear their seeds inside pods and have distinctive five-petalled flowers.

Peacock A colourful butterfly with yellow, black and blue markings forming an eye spot on each of its predominantly red wings. These 'eyes' look like the markings on a male peacock's tail feathers, and give the butterfly its name.

Peacock worm A bristle worm belonging to a small group known as fanworms. Its name comes from the shape of its tufted tentacles; it is also called a feather-duster worm. The peacock worm lives on the sandy sea bed, making a tube in which to live. The branched, feathery tentacles reach out from the tube, waving about in the water to trap food.

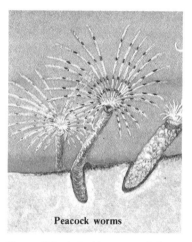

Peacock worms

Pear, wild A deciduous tree belonging to the rose family, found on the edges of woodlands and along hedgerows. It is the ancestor of all cultivated varieties, and can grow as tall as 18 metres.

Pearlwort Several low, tufted, flowering plants related to the stitchworts and campions. The most common species is the procumbent pearlwort. It is a small creeping plant with long leafy stems that spring from a basal rosette of slender leaves.

Peewit See LAPWING.

Pelagic Inhabiting the open sea, away from the shore and the sea bed. The word can also be used for animals living in the middle of large lakes.

Pen (1) A female swan. (2) A horny strip inside the body of a squid. It gives support to the soft body.

Penicillium A green, mat-forming mould that grows on bread, overripe fruit and many other foods. It can grow in drier places than many other moulds. Spores are formed all over the surface. The mould produces penicillin, the antibiotic that is used in medicine to fight germs.

Pennycress Several species of flowering plant belonging to the cabbage family. Like other members of the family they have small, four-petalled flowers borne in a stalked spike. The fruits are small rounded pods with broad flat wings either side, making them look heart-shaped.

Peppered moth A geometer moth that rests mainly on tree trunks by day. There are two forms: one is the

1800s when factory smoke blackened the trees in industrial areas, making these moths difficult to see against the dark bark. They therefore escaped being eaten by birds and in time became the most abundant form. But with cleaner air and cleaner trees, the speckled peppered moth is again becoming more numerous.

Perch Family of freshwater fishes that includes, along with the common perch, the zander and ruffe. Members have two dorsal fins, the front one of which is very spiny. The common perch is one of the most abundant, and is found in lowland lakes and rivers. It is about 25 cm long with red fins on its tail and the underside of its body. It feeds on smaller fish and water animals.

Perching bird The Passeriformes or perching birds include about half the bird species. They all have a backward-pointing toe.

Perennial Any plant that lives for more than two years.

Perianth The outer part of a flower, comprising the corolla (petals) and the calyx (sepals).

Peppered moth

Periwinkle

original form, speckled black and white; the other is totally black. The black form became common in the

Periwinkle (1) A creeping evergreen plant that scrambles over the ground in woods and hedges, putting down roots from its stem. The lesser periwinkle has violet, five-petalled flowers and oval, leathery leaves. The greater periwinkle has larger flowers, broader leaves, and stems that take root only at the tip. Both species prefer shady places. (2) A type of WINKLE.

Petal One of the colourful outer parts of a flower, which help to attract pollinating insects. Lines and other patterns on the petals often guide the insects to the nectar, leading them past the stamens and stigmas on the way.

Petiole (1) The stalk of a leaf. (2) The narrow 'waist' of bees, wasps, and ants.

Phalarope Small water birds related to sandpipers. They live mostly at sea and nest by coastal marshes and lakes.

Pheasant Large birds with colourful plumages and long tails, which forage for insects on the ground (in the same way as poultry). The male bird is much more colourful than the female.

Photosynthesis The food-making process of green plants. It can take place only in the light. The green substance chlorophyll absorbs light and uses the energy to make glucose sugar from water and carbon dioxide gas. Oxygen is given off in the process.

Phylum The largest category used in the classification of animals. All members of a phylum have basically the same structure, although they may differ greatly in size and in detailed appearance. The largest of all the thirty or so phyla is the Arthropoda.

Piddock Several species of marine bivalve mollusc which bore into rocks, clay or mud. Most live in shallow water. At one end of each valve the piddock has rows of toothed cutting edges which, as the shells rock back and forth, form a hole. Some piddocks can drill down several times the length of their own shell. Piddocks feed on food particles floating in sea water.

Pied woodpecker See SPOTTED WOOD-PECKER.

Pigeon A group of almost 300 species of seed-eating bird, of which five are commonly found in Europe. The pigeon group includes the doves. In fact, the word 'pigeon' and 'dove' are used very loosely, and there is no real difference between the two kinds. Pigeons are plump birds with small heads. They can fly quickly and are often used for

Feral pigeon

Rock dove

racing. Most of them eat only seeds and fruit, though some species like insects. All pigeons have deep cooing or booming voices, and a repetitive song. See COLLARED DOVE, STOCK DOVE, ROCK DOVE, TURTLE DOVE and WOOD PIGEON.

Pigment Any colouring material in a plant or animal. Examples include CHLOROPHYLL (green) and MELANIN (brown).

Pike A freshwater fish commonly found in lakes and slow-running rivers throughout Europe except the Mediterranean region. It is a long-bodied fish, with a flat, broad snout and the dorsal fin set well back on the body. An adult pike is about 40 cm long, but long-lived specimens have been known to reach a length of 1.5 metres. Pike are notorious predators, and can take fish up to half their own weight. They also prey on water voles, frogs, young ducks and moorhens.

Pike-perch See ZANDER.

Pilchard A marine fish, up to 25 cm long, related to the herring. It is found in large shoals in the Atlantic and the Mediterranean, but its range does not extend further north than southern England.

Scots pine

regions further south. Their slender, almost cylindrical needles are borne in bunches of two, three or five, according to species. The trees are evergreen and are commonly planted for their timber or for ornament. The Scots pine is a common species, growing up to 35 metres high.

Pilchard

Pimpernel Low flowering plants belonging to the primrose family. The plants have tiny, five-petalled flowers which only open in the sunshine, giving them their alternative name of poor man's weatherglass.

Pine A group of cone-bearing trees with needle-shaped leaves, found mainly in the cooler northern parts of the world and in mountainous

Pine vole, common The smallest of the voles, only 8.5 cm long, found in central Europe. It burrows more than the other voles and spends much of the time underground, feeding on roots and bulbs. It lives in grassland and open woods.

Pink A group of flowering plants related to the campions and catchflies. Pinks have four or five, usually notched or ragged petals, beneath which the sepals are fused to form a tube. The flowers may be pink, white or red, and the leaves are greyish-green and slender.

Pin mould There are several similar kinds of pin mould, so named because their spore capsules, raised on slender stalks, resemble tiny pins. The fluffy mycelium grows on dung, as well as bread and many other foods. Pin mould is also known by its Latin name, Mucor. See picture on page 120.

Pintail A dabbling duck with long, pointed tail feathers in the male. He has a brown head and neck, grey back and white throat and belly. The female is speckled brown. Pintails live on fresh water, and on moors and marshes, or on coastal waters in winter.

Pipefish Member of a group of tubular marine fishes with bony external skeletons. Pipefishes live among seaweed in shallow coastal waters and feed on other animals such as shrimps. The largest pipefish is about 60 cm long.

birds. The slightly larger rock pipit of sea coasts is greyer in colour.

Pistil The complete female part of a flower, consisting of one or more carpels (including styles, stigmas and ovaries).

Plaice The commonest flatfish in European waters. It lives on the sea bed and grows to a length of 55 cm. Its upper side is commonly grey-brown with red spots though the fish can change colour to some extent to match the colour of its background.

Plane A family of deciduous trees frequently seen in cities. They have deeply lobed, fan-shaped leaves and their flowers and round fruits hang in clusters. There are six species but that most commonly grown is the

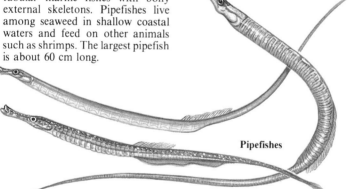

Pipefishes

Pipistrelle The smallest and most abundant bat in Europe, only 3.5 cm long. It forms large colonies in buildings such as churches, and is seen in considerable numbers when flying to its winter roosting places in caves and mines.

Pipit Birds related to the wagtail, with a similar jaunty running motion. The meadow pipit and tree pipit are speckled brownish-yellow

London plane – a hybrid (cross) between an American species and the Oriental plane. This tree can grow in the hard ground under paving-stones and can tolerate polluted air. It grows to a height of 35 metres.

Plankton Free-floating plant and animal life in the surface waters of seas and large lakes. The plant life, consisting of millions of tiny plants, is called phytoplankton. It uses energy from the sun to make organic matter in a process known as photosynthesis. A host of tiny animals, the zooplankton, feeds on the phytoplankton. Zooplankton is made up of many one-celled creatures such as radiolarians, along with tiny jellyfishes, snails and worms, young fishes, and vast numbers of small crustaceans and their larvae.

Plantain A family of mainly wind-pollinated flowering plants that are widespread in grassy places or by the sea. Plantains have dense spikes of tiny green or brown flowers with prominent stamens. The veined or ridged leaves form a rosette at the base of the stem. The ribwort

European polecat

plantain is one of the commonest flowering plants in Europe.

Plant kingdom A typical plant cannot move, has no nervous system, has cellulose cell walls and feeds on inorganic matter. See the diagram of the plant kingdom on page 192.

Plant louse See APHID.

Plover Long-legged wading birds, often found near the seashore, but also seen on farmland and moors. The plovers include the grey, ringed, golden and Kentish plovers, and also the DOTTEREL and LAPWING. Plovers feed on worms, insects and

small water animals such as shrimps. Unlike many waders, they have short bills.

Plumage The feathery coat of a bird.

Plume moth A group of ghostly-looking insects whose wings are divided into feathery plumes. There are white and brown plume moths.

Pochard A bird belonging to the duck family. Pochards feed on water plants and small water creatures, finding their food by diving. The male pochard is mostly grey, with a chestnut head and black breast. The female is mostly brown.

Polecat A nocturnal carnivore closely related to the stoat and found over most of Europe except the north. It is about 40 cm long, with a long tail and short legs. Its coat is made up of long brown hairs with woolly yellow under-fur. Polecats can produce an unpleasant, strong smell from musk glands at the base of the tail. They live mainly in light wooded areas and are often found near water.

Pollack A marine fish closely related to the saithe and belonging to the cod group. The pollack (or pollock) is generally found close to the coast.

Pollen The mass of dust-like spores produced in the stamens of flowers. These spores are the male reproductive bodies and they must reach the stigmas of the right kinds of flowers before seeds can be formed. The transfer of pollen to the stigmas is called POLLINATION. Pollen is also produced by the male cones of pines and other coniferous trees.

Pollination The transfer of pollen from the stamens to the stigmas of a flower – either the same flower or a different flower of the same kind – which results in fertilization and the formation of seeds. Most flowers actually have some method of discouraging self-pollination – often by having the stamens and stigmas ripening at different times. The flowers then have to be cross-pollinated with pollen from another flower, which is much better for the plants because it usually produces stronger offspring.

When a pollen grain lands on a ripe stigma of the right kind it sends out a slender tube which grows down through the stigma into the carpel. Minute cells from the pollen grain pass down the tube and one of them fertilizes an ovule in the carpel. The fertilized ovule then develops into a seed.

Polyp The tubular or cup-shaped stage in the life cycle of most coelenterates. A polyp is usually fixed to one spot. Sea anemones and corals are polyps, and so is the freshwater *Hydra.*

Polypore See BRACKET FUNGUS.

Pondskater A group of long-legged water bugs that 'skate' over the surface of ponds and streams. They

Pondskater

use only two pairs of legs for motion; the front pair are used as claws to catch the dead or dying insects on which the pondskaters feed.

Pond snail Several species of gastropod mollusc found in freshwater pools and streams. They have spiral shells ending in a point, and do not swim, but crawl about underwater feeding on pond weed. They also eat fish eggs.

Great pond snail

Pondweed A group of aquatic flowering plants that grow in still or slow-flowing fresh water. They have spikes of tiny green, petalless flowers and a variety of leaf shapes, from long and slender to broad and flat. A few species have floating leaves and flowers borne above the surface.

Pony A horse of less than 14 hands (140 cm) high. Few European ponies are truly wild; they are mostly domestic varieties that are left to roam wild.

Poor man's weather-glass See PIMPERNEL.

Pope See RUFFE.

Poplar A group of deciduous trees belonging to the willow family. Poplars are fast-growing and can withstand strong gales, for which reason they are frequently grown as windbreaks along roadsides. Most have triangular leaves. Their flowers, arranged as catkins, are single-sexed and borne on separate trees.

Poppy A family of plants whose bright red or yellow flowers add a vivid splash of colour to cornfields and wasteland. The four large petals often have a wrinkled appearance, and the stems contain a milky white juice. The common poppy has

Poppy

bright red petals and black stamens. Its leaves and stem are covered in stiff hairs and its seed pods are almost round. The yellow horned poppy is a yellow-petalled species often found on shingle by the sea. It is hairless and has extremely long seed pods, up to 30 cm long.

Porbeagle A fast, strong-swimming shark that grows up to 3 metres long. It feeds mostly on shoaling fishes near the surface and often raids fisheries, causing great damage by ripping the nets.

Portuguese man-o'-war A jellyfish with a blue or pink float and sail, frequently carried to northern European waters by the Gulf Stream. It stuns fishes with its stinging tentacles, which trail for up to 2 metres.

Potter wasp A wasp named for the clay cells or 'pots' which it builds for its larvae. The pot is fixed to a plant stem and stocked with caterpillars paralysed by the wasp's sting. The wasp larvae feed on the caterpillars.

Powan See WHITEFISH.

Prawn A group of crustaceans related to the shrimps but usually bigger. Like shrimps, prawns have hunched backs, long antennae and small claws. They scuttle about the sea bed, often hiding in the sand and coming out to feed at night. When startled, they shoot backwards through the water at great speed.

Predator Any animal that eats or preys on another. The owl, for example, is a predator of rats and mice.

Primrose A common flowering plant that often forms thick patches in woods and on waysides. It has solitary yellow, five-petalled flowers borne on softly hairy stems, and the long oval leaves grow straight from the roots.

Proboscis (1) The slender tongue of butterflies and moths, used for sucking nectar from flowers. (2) The spongy, mop-like tongue of house-flies and bluebottles.

Proboscis worm See RIBBON WORM.

Processionary moth A group of moths whose caterpillars often march in single file procession to feed at night. The caterpillars of the pine processionary live in pine trees, grouped together in silken nests where they spend the winter. The larvae pupate in spring and emerge as adult moths. Another kind of processionary moth feeds on oak trees.

Proleg One of the stumpy legs on the rear half of a caterpillar's body. It bears many minute hooks which help the caterpillar to cling tightly to its food plant.

Prosoma See SPIDER.

Prothallus See ALTERNATION OF GENERATIONS.

Protoplasm The living contents of a plant or animal cell, comprising the nucleus and the other contents (the cytoplasm). Protoplasm is a translucent, colourless substance.

Protozoan Any of the many very tiny animals whose bodies consist of just a single cell. Very few can be seen with the naked eye. Most live in watery surroundings and many move about by waving minute hairs.

Pseudopodium One of the temporary 'arms' of an AMOEBA or similar organism, put out for feeding or for moving along.

Ptarmigan A game bird related to the grouse. It lives on mountains and northern tundra, and in winter its sandy-grey plumage changes to almost completely white. Ptarmigans eat seeds, mosses and other plant food. The nest is a hollow on the ground.

Pteridophyte Any member of a large group of flowerless plants that includes ferns, horsetails and clubmosses. These plants all reproduce by scattering dust-like spores. There are no seeds.

Puffball One of a group of almost spherical fungi containing a mass of dark spores, and attached to the ground by a slender thread. The skin of the ball generally splits to form a small hole when ripe, and the spores are puffed out in clouds when the fungus is touched. Even a falling raindrop can cause them to shoot out. The giant puffball grows up to 30 cm across.

Puffin A bird of sea coasts and islands, related to the auks. It is a stout bird with black and white plumage and short legs. The puffin's large, yellow bill becomes gaudily coloured – grey, blue, scarlet and yellow – in summer. It eats small fishes and lives in colonies on sea cliffs. The nest is often a burrow, either an old rabbit hole, or one dug out by the puffin itself.

Pupa The stage in the life history of many insects during which the adult body is formed from that of the larva. The pupa may be able to move, but it never feeds. Insects passing through a pupal stage include bees and wasps, beetles, flies, and butterflies and moths. The pupa of a butterfly or moth is commonly called a chrysalis.

Purple emperor

Purple emperor A large butterfly which spends most of its time flying around oak trees. It may also be attracted to muddy pools or to dead animals. The male's wings have a rich purple sheen when seen from certain angles; the female has brownish upper wings marked with white. The caterpillars feed on sallow (pussy willow).

Purslane The name given to several unrelated groups of flowering plants. Pink purslane belongs to the same family as SPRING BEAUTY, but grows in damp woods. Water purslane is related to purple loosestrife. It has paired oval leaves

Puffball

and creeps over wet ground. The sea purslane belongs to the goosefoot family. It is a short silvery undershrub of salt-marshes, and has small green flowers in short spikes.

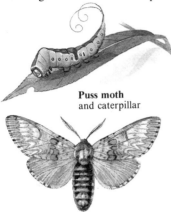

Puss moth
and caterpillar

Puss moth A furry grey moth with a somewhat cat-like head when seen from above. Even more striking is the puss moth caterpillar. For defence, it draws back its head into its red neck and displays two waving red 'tails', making itself look both larger and fiercer than it really is.

Pygmy shrew A small shrew, only 5 cm long, that lives in northern and central Europe.

Pygmy shrew

Q

Quail The smallest of the European game birds, related to the partridge. It has streaky brown plumage with a striped head and small tail. Quails are shy birds and prefer to keep to the ground, hiding among crops and grasses. They feed on seeds and insects and migrate south for the winter.

Quaking grass Several species of grass found throughout Europe. The most common species are the small quaking grass, pearl grass and the widespread common quaking grass. They are named after their rounded spikelets of tiny flowers which quiver or quake in the wind. The grasses are often planted for ornamental purposes.

R

Rabbit A mammal closely related to the hare but with shorter hind legs and ears. It is about 45 cm long. Rabbits originated in Spain but have spread throughout most of western Europe. They are grazing animals and, as such, like to live in grasslands, preferably near trees, where they dig extensive burrows or warrens. The females produce up to six large litters a year.

Rabbitfish See CHIMAERA.

Radula The horny tongue of slugs and snails. It is covered with tiny teeth and rasps away at the animal's food like a file or a strip of sandpaper. The front end is always wearing away, but the radula keeps growing from the base, rather like fingernails, and pushing new rows of teeth forward.

Ragged robin A flowering plant closely related to the campion. The pink flowers are characterized by their finely divided petals which give them a ragged appearance. The sepals are fused to form a tube beneath the flower, and the oval leaves grow in opposite pairs. The plant is often found on wet ground.

Ragworm Segmented worms of the sandy seashore. Ragworms are bristle worms but look rather like centipedes. They are found in a variety of colours. They leave their burrows to roam around hunting for food. Most ragworms are carnivorous.

Ragwort Several much-branched plants of the daisy family, with yellow daisy-like flowers. The leaves are often deeply lobed, giving a ragged appearance. The common ragwort is widespread in dry grassland and is often found covered with the gold and black caterpillars of the CINNABAR MOTH.

Rail Birds with long legs and short tails, belonging to the same family as the coot and crakes. Rails are shy, secretive birds and seldom fly. Their plumage is predominently brown with darker streaks. The widespread water rail usually hides among the reeds of marshes, fens and lakesides. It has a long red bill and a black and white barred belly. The similar land rail, also known as the

corncrake, has a shorter, pale brown bill and chestnut wing patches. It lives in grassy fields and meadows and its call is a loud 'crake'.

Ram's horn snail A gastropod mollusc that lives in fresh water. It has a flattened spiral shell, deep reddish-brown in colour, which resembles the coiled horn of a ram. It lives in ponds and slow-moving streams, feeding on waterweed and algae.

Ramsons A small flowering plant of the lily family. It has a three-ridged stem and white, six-petalled, star-shaped flowers which are arranged in a delicate cluster at the tip of the stalk. Its broad leaves smell of garlic. Ramsons are often found carpeting woodlands.

Rape A flowering plant of the cabbage family, closely related to swede. It has dull greyish leaves and yellow flowers arranged in a spike.

Raspberry A shrub belonging to the rose family, widely cultivated for its fruit. The woody stems bear small prickles and the white, five-petalled flowers are small and rather inconspicuous. In the wild, raspberries usually grow in shaded areas such as in woods and among bushes.

Rat A medium-sized rodent with large naked ears and a long, almost

Black rat

Brown rat

naked tail. Two species are commonly found in Europe: the black and the brown rat. The black or ship rat is the smaller of the two species, only 20 cm long. Its colour varies from black to brown. The brown rat is common throughout Europe. It is 24 cm long and is sometimes black. Its ears are smaller than those of its cousin.

Raven The largest of all the crows, with a black plumage. Ravens are good fliers, and usually live on mountains or sea cliffs. The raven feeds on carrion, small animals, eggs, insects and fruit. Its call is a harsh 'croak'.

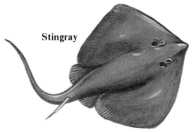

Stingray

Ray Member of a group of cartilaginous fishes related to the sharks. Rays have flat bodies with huge fins which give them their diamond shape. They use these fins to propel themselves through the water. Most species produce their eggs in horny cases called 'mermaids' purses'. There are about 250 species of ray, of which about 20 are found in European waters. It is also called the rock ray. See also SKATE.

Razorbill A seabird similar in appearance to its close relative, the guillemot, but with a much broader bill. It is black with white underparts and has a white stripe across its black bill. Razorbills spend most of their lives at sea, diving to catch fishes, and only come ashore to breed.

Razorshell A bivalve mollusc named after the old-fashioned 'cut-throat' razor. Its valves are hinged near one end only. Razorshells grow to some 15 cm, and usually lie buried up to 1 metre down in the mud. They dig their burrows with a long, fleshy 'foot'.

Receptacle The base of a flower from which all the parts, sepals, petals, stamens and carpels, rise.

Red admiral A colourful butterfly with red and white markings on a velvety black background. Red admirals migrate from the south into northern Europe in the spring. They breed here but do not survive the cold winters. The caterpillars feed on stinging nettles.

Redd The breeding place of the salmon, in a gravelly river bed with a moderate current flowing over it. The female salmon uses her tail to dig a hollow (the redd) in the gravel in which to lay her eggs.

Red deer A deer found in isolated places all over Europe. It stands up to 1.4 metres high at the shoulder and is the largest deer except for the elk. It has a red-brown summer coat that turns greyish in winter. Red deer feed on grass, young shoots, leaves and acorns.

Redpoll A bird belonging to the finch family, which lives mainly in forests of birch, alder and conifers. It has a red forehead and a small black

Redpoll

bib; breeding males also have reddish breasts. Redpolls nest in trees and bushes and roam in large flocks in winter.

Redshank Wading birds named for their reddish legs. The common redshank lives on coastal shores, marshes and mud-flats. It has a grey-brown back and streaked, pale underparts, long legs and a long slim bill. Its diet includes insects, shellfish and crustaceans. The closely related greenshank is a bird with similar habits and appearance but it has greenish legs.

Red spider mite A small, plant-feeding arachnid, which does serious damage to orchards.

easily distinguished by the rich chestnut-red streaks on its sides. Redwings fly from the north to southern and western Europe for the winter, where they form large flocks. They are frequently associated with fieldfares.

Reed Several species of tall water-side grasses which cover huge areas of ground, forming reed-beds. Reeds have tough stems that survive throughout the winter, and broad leaves. The flowerheads are purple and plume-like. Reed stems are used for thatching.

Reed bunting A ground-nesting bird which prefers wet marshy land but will also live in drier places. The

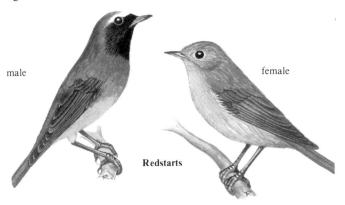

male

female

Redstarts

Redstart One of the smaller members of the thrush family. The birds visit Europe from April to October, spending the winter in central Africa. Both sexes have the red tail that gives the bird its name but only the male has a russet-coloured breast. They are found in woodlands and gardens. Black redstarts have reddish tails like ordinary redstarts but are otherwise much darker. They are commonly found in towns.

Redwing A bird that looks similar to its relative, the song thrush, but is

birds are readily identified by their white collars and the male's black head and throat. They have a monotonous four-note song.

Reedmace See BULRUSH.

Reed warbler A small bird that lives and nests mostly among reeds, close to water. It is rusty-brown with paler underparts. Reed warblers nest in colonies with their nests slung from plant stems, clear of the ground. The birds are summer visitors from Africa.

Regeneration (1) The replacement of

lost parts by living organisms. (2) The regrowth of a woodland after fire or felling.

Reindeer The most common deer of the extreme north, found mostly in Lapland. There are a few wild herds but most reindeer are now domesticated. Wild animals are pale grey in winter, greyish-brown in summer. They stand over 1 metre tall at the shoulder and, unlike other deer, both sexes have antlers. In winter they feed on lichens known as reindeer moss, and in summer they feed on grass.

Reproduction The production of young plants or animals by older ones. Sexual reproduction involves the joining of male and female cells to produce the new generation. This is the commonest form of reproduction in both plants and animals.

Non-sexual or asexual reproduction does not involve any joining of cells. Bacteria and many protozoans reproduce merely by splitting in two when they reach a certain size. Each half then grows up and repeats the process.

Reptile Any member of a group of

Elk

bull

cow

Reindeer

bull

cow

backboned animals that includes snakes and lizards, tortoises, and crocodiles. They are all air-breathing animals, although many live in the water, and they are all covered with scales. All are cold-blooded and they are active only in warm weather. Most of the 6000 or so species alive today live in the warmer parts of the world. The dinosaurs that roamed the world 100 million years ago were also reptiles.

Respiration The process of taking in oxygen and giving out carbon dioxide. Most land animals use lungs to breathe air, while most aquatic animals use gills to extract oxygen from water.

Restharrow Several species of low-growing woody plant belonging to the pea family. They have usually pink pea-like flowers arranged in spikes, hairy stems and leaves, and long thin seed pods.

Rhizoid A simple root belonging to a moss or a liverwort, consisting of just a few cells, with no special channels for carrying water.

Rhizome A horizontal stem growing on or under the ground and lasting for at least two growing seasons. It sends up new aerial shoots at intervals.

Rhododendron A large evergreen shrub, bearing bowl-shaped flowers in a range of colours, from rich purples to white. They grow in acid soils, even at high altitudes.

Ribbon worm Also called proboscis worms, ribbon worms are the simplest form of animal to have both a digestive system and blood moving through veins. Most ribbon worms are long and thin. Some grow to several metres. They live mostly in mud burrows on the sea bed, but some live in fresh water. They catch prey by firing out a tube-like proboscis which spears or entangles the victim.

Ring dove See WOOD PIGEON.

Ringlet One of the brown butterflies, with pale 'eye' marks or ringlets on the underside of its dark brown wings. It is usually seen flying in summer across hedgerows and woodland clearings.

Ring ouzel A black bird belonging to the thrush family. It can be distinguished from the blackbird by a white bib across the breast. The females tend to be browner than the males. Ring ouzels are found on moors and mountains, especially where there are a few trees.

Roach A freshwater fish belonging to the carp family. It is silvery in colour and the adult fish has red fins. It lives in shoals in lakes and slow-running streams all over Europe, and feeds on plants and slower moving animals.

Roach

Dace

Robber-fly A group of true flies, also known as assassin-flies. These large flies are expert hunters of other insects, and are capable of seizing bees on the wing. With their dagger-like mouth parts, robber-flies stab their prey and suck out the body juices.

Robin One of the most familiar birds of the thrush family, with its distinctive red breast and brown upper parts. Robins usually live alone, each male and female bird fiercely jealous of its own territory, except when they pair during the breeding season.

Robin

Rockcress Several species of low, flowering plant belonging to the cabbage family. They have small white, four-petalled flowers arranged in stalked spikes.

Rock dove The ancestor of racing pigeons and the feral pigeons so commonly seen in cities. Rock doves live near cliffs, where they make their nests in caves and hollows. Feral pigeons are domesticated pigeons which have become wild again.

Rocket The name given to several species of flowering plant belonging to the cabbage family. The sea rocket is commonly found growing close to the high tide mark.

Rockling One of several species of bottom-living fish belonging to the cod group. Rocklings have long fins running most of the length of the back and belly. There is one barbel on the lower jaw and several above the mouth.

Rock-rose Several low undershrubs with five-petalled, rose-like flowers. They are not related to the true roses. The common rock-rose has usually yellow flowers and small, untoothed leaves. It grows on chalky soils and is often cultivated in gardens. All species produce egg-shaped fruits.

Rock salmon See DOGFISH.

Rodent Any of a group of mammals that includes rats and mice. These animals are all basically vegetarians and all have large chisel-like teeth at the front of the mouth. They can gnaw through very hard materials, and the teeth grow continuously to make up for wear at the tip.

Roe deer Smallest of Europe's native deer, found in most parts of Europe except Ireland. It stands about 70 cm high at the shoulder and has a short, red-brown summer coat with a distinctive white rump; the winter coat is longer and greyer. Roe deer live in woodlands, either alone or in pairs, and they feed at night.

Rook A bird belonging to the crow family, with black plumage and a patch of greyish-white skin around the beak. The rook's bare face and its 'shaggy trousers' distinguish it from its slightly larger cousin the carrion crow. Rooks live near farmland, nesting in tree-top colonies. They have many different calls, and eat grain and caterpillars.

Root The part of a plant that anchors it in the ground and absorbs water and minerals from the soil. Most of these nutrients are absorbed by minute hairs, found only on the youngest and finest parts of the root system. Some plants have just one main root, known as a tap-root, with a few small branches, but others have numerous roots growing out from the base of the stem and branching in all directions.

Rose A large group of flowering shrubs, widely cultivated for their colourful, fragrant blooms. Roses have thorny stems and white, pink or red, five-petalled flowers (though cultivars may have more petals and different colours). The toothed leaves are divided into leaflets and the plants bear a berry-like fruit called a hip. Wild roses include the dog rose and the field rose, both of

Dog rose

which grow in hedgerows and scrub. The roses belong to a large family of plants which contains many trees, shrubs and herbs, such as apples, brambles and cinquefoils.

Rotifer A group of tiny animals that move through the water by means of a spinning 'wheel' of hairs. Another name for the animal is the wheel animalcule. Rotifers live mainly in fresh water but a few species live on damp moss or in the sea.

Rough hound See DOGFISH.

Roundworm See NEMATODE.

Rove beetle A group of large hunting and scavenging beetles whose long wings are elaborately folded away beneath very short wing covers,

leaving most of the body uncovered. The DEVIL'S COACH HORSE belongs to this family.

Rowan A deciduous tree belonging to the rose family, also known as mountain ash. It grows up to 20 metres tall and its hardiness makes it popular in town gardens. It produces creamy-white flowers, and round red berries which are made into jelly.

Rowan

Royal jelly See HONEY BEE.

Ruby-tailed wasp Several species belonging to a group of insects called cuckoo wasps, named for the females' habit of laying their eggs in the nests of other insects. They are not closely related to the true wasps. Most ruby-tailed wasps have red, or ruby abdomens. They choose the nest of a solitary bee or wasp in which to lay their egg. The larva hatches quickly and eats not only the host's food but also the host's egg or larva.

Rudd A freshwater fish with bright red fins, belonging to the carp family and found in slow-running rivers and shallow lakes. It is about 25 cm long and lives in shoals, feeding on insects, snails and waterweed.

Ruff A wading bird of the seashore. The male bird displays during the breeding season by extending a ruff or collar of feathers around its neck. The female has no ruff, and is called a reeve. Ruffs are speckled grey-brown birds, similar to redshanks in general appearance.

Ruffe A freshwater fish also called the pope. It is similar to its relative the perch but smaller, and lacks the red fins on the tail and underside of the body.

Ruminant Any mammal that chews the cud. Deer, sheep, goats and cows are ruminants. They are all grazing or browsing animals with multi-chambered stomachs.

Runner A slender, fast-growing horizontal or arching stem that takes root at its tip and produces a new plant. The runner then rots away, leaving the new plant quite independent of the parent. Strawberries produce many new plants in this way.

Rush A group of tall flowering plants, commonly found in clumps at the water's edge. The rushes have long hollow or pith-filled stems, and clusters of tiny brown or green flowers. Some species have no leaves. The dried stems are commonly woven into baskets. The flowering rush is an unrelated plant with long, slim leaves and clusters of bright pink, six-petalled flowers. It grows by fresh water. The BULRUSHES or cattails are also unrelated; they belong to the reedmace group of plants.

Rut The mating season of the deer, during which the males often roar and bellow and frequently fight. The red deer rut occurs in the autumn, when the stags round up as many females as they can and defend them against other males.

S

St George's mushroom A large grassland toadstool with a smooth cap that is white at the edges and pale buff in the centre.

St John's wort A large group of herbaceous plants with yellow five-petalled flowers. The oval leaves grow in pairs and have almost transparent veins. Some species, such as the evergreen, creeping rose of Sharon, are cultivated. The common St John's wort has transparent dots on its leaves.

Slender St John's wort

St Mark's-fly A dark hairy fly which emerges on or around St Mark's Day, 25th April. These flies often form swarms over grassland.

St Mark's-fly

Saithe A fish of the open sea, belonging to the cod group and also known as the coley or coalfish. It has three dorsal fins and grows up to 130 cm long. Saithe live in shoals, unlike most other members of the cod group.

Salamander A tailed amphibian that lives in cool, damp places. Many species return to the water to breed; there they either lay eggs or give birth to tadpoles. Other species lay their eggs on land; the tadpoles develop inside the eggs and hatch out as small adults. The fire salamander is a common species found all over Europe except the British Isles and Scandinavia. It is about 20 cm long including the tail, and has a striking yellow and black coloration that warns its enemies that it has a poisonous skin and is inedible.

Salmon

spend from one to four years at sea, feeding and growing rapidly. Then they return to the same clear, upland stream where they hatched out, battling upstream against often fierce currents. Upon arrival, each female digs a hollow or redd in the gravel of the river bed, and lays her eggs in it. Most males and many females die after spawning, but some fish return to the sea and may make a second, and in rare cases a third journey up the rivers. The salmon reaches a length of about 150 cm and, like other members of its family, has a small fleshy fin on its underside, just in front of the tail.

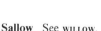
Fire salamander

Sallow See WILLOW.

Salmon A fish related to the trout, that breeds in fresh water but spends much of its life at sea. Exactly where salmon go in the oceans is still not fully understood, though they have been caught up to 2700 km away from their native waters. The fish

Salsify A flowering plant of the daisy family. It is sometimes known as the oyster plant because its roots taste of oysters. It is widespread on grassland, and up to a metre high. It has solitary purple flowerheads made up of long ray FLORETS surrounded by equally long sepal-like bracts.

Samphire A name given to several unrelated flowering plants that are usually found growing on sea cliffs or around the coastline. The rock samphire is a member of the carrot family with clusters of small, pale yellow flowers and fleshy lobed leaves. The golden samphire is another fleshy plant, belonging to the daisy family. Its flowers are arranged in a flat-topped cluster.

Sand-eel Member of a group of small eel-like fishes which are rarely seen, but which exist in huge numbers. At least five species live in European waters.

Sanderling A small wading bird, usually found in flocks along sandy shores and mudflats. It is pale grey and white in winter plumage, changing to reddish-brown and white in summer. It runs rapidly over the sand, hunting for sand-hoppers and other small animals.

Sand hopper

Sand hopper A group of small crustaceans that live in and around water. Sand hoppers are amphipods and they look like small shrimps that have been flattened from side to side. On the seashore they are commonly found hopping about among seaweed at the tidal zone.

Sand lizard A relative of the green lizard, found over most of Europe except the extreme north and south, and very rare in Britain. It is about 22 cm long including the tail, and varies in colour from bright green to reddish brown. It lives mainly in dry areas.

Sandpiper Wading birds, usually seen around lakes and marshes and, especially when migrating, in flocks near the coast. The common sandpiper is a brown bird, with white underparts. It has a characteristic bobbing motion as it wades through the water or perches on low objects. Other species include the wood sandpiper and green sand-piper. Sandpipers feed on insects, worms and small crustaceans.

Sand star See BRITTLE STAR.

Sand urchin See SEA POTATO.

Sand wasp A family of solitary wasps which provide their young with a food store of paralysed caterpillars. The female stings the prey, rendering it helpless, and drags it into her burrow in the sand. She lays a single egg on the caterpillar, which provides the sand wasp larva with a ready-to-eat food supply when it hatches. Sand wasps are slender insects, with very thin 'waists'.

Sanicle A flowering plant of the carrot family which forms thick carpets in woodlands. It is a hairless plant with shiny ivy-like leaves borne on long stalks. Its pinkish or white flowers are arranged in umbrella-shaped clusters.

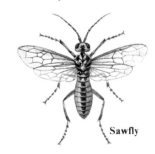

Sawfly

Sawfly A group of insects related to the bees and wasps, which get their name from the saw-like cutting edge of the ovipositor (egg-laying organ).

The female uses her ovipositor to saw holes in plant stems into which she deposits her eggs. Sawfly larvae eat greedily and can damage trees and garden plants.

Golden saxifrage

Saxifrage A large group of flowering plants, most of which grow in rocky places on cliffs and mountains. Many are squat plants with rosettes of leaves around the base of the stem, and most have small white flowers.

Scabious Several species of flowering plant related to the teasel. They have hairy stems and leaves and their small, mostly blue flowers are tightly packed into a head, similar to a composite flowerhead. The common devilsbit scabious is found in damp places and gets its curious name from its short root which is said to have been bitten off by the devil.

Scale A flat horny outgrowth of the skin, found in fishes and reptiles and also on the legs of birds.

Scale insect A group of bugs that feed by sucking sap from plants. The females of many species are covered by horny scales. Only the males have wings. The wingless females do not move, but remain fixed to their food plant. Like greenfly, these insects can be harmful pests.

Scaleworm A group of marine bristle worms with arched backs covered in pairs of overlapping

scales. The trunk-like snout has feelers and horny jaws. An example of a scaleworm is the SEA MOUSE.

Scallop A family of marine bivalve molluscs which, unlike other bivalves such as oysters, can swim. They do so by shooting jets of water out of their shells.

Scarab beetle A group of dung beetles that are useful scavengers, disposing of animal droppings by burying and eating them. The sacred scarab has a gleaming black body. It collects dung into neat balls and rolls them about. Then it buries the balls and eats them. Females also lay their eggs on them so that the larvae have a ready food supply.

Sacred scarab beetle

Schneider A small freshwater fish belonging to the carp family and found in clear streams and lakes in central Europe.

Scops owl An owl which gets its name from a Greek word meaning 'little horned owl'. It is a small bird with prominent ear tufts that look rather like cats' ears. It lives in southern Europe, but sometimes is found as far north as the British Isles, especially in spring.

Scorpion fly A group of lacy-winged insects, with long antennae, and jaws at the end of their stout beaks. Scorpion flies get their name from the way in which the male's body is

149

Scorpion fly

curled over at the end like a scorpion's tail. They are scavengers, feeding on the bodies of dead insects and other waste matter.

Scoter Ducks which live mainly on seashores, occasionally visiting inland waters. The male common scoter is black, the female brown. They feed on shellfish and some crustaceans.

Screech owl See SCOPS OWL and BARN OWL.

Sculpin Member of a large family of fishes, most of which live in the sea. Sculpins are small, with large heads and mouths, and many of them have spines on their heads. They have no scales, just a few warty projections on their smooth skins. Sculpins are bottom-living fishes. One group, the BULLHEADS, lives mostly in fresh water. Its members tend to be smaller than their sea-dwelling relatives.

Scurvy grass This plant is not in fact a grass, but a member of the cabbage family. It has fleshy, heart-shaped leaves and loose spikes of white or lilac, star-shaped flowers. There are several species, most of which are found in salt-marshes or muddy shores.

Sea anemone A group of marine animals which belong to the same phylum as the jellyfishes – the coelenterates. Sea anemones have soft tubular bodies and a mouth fringed with tentacles. Stinging cells on the tentacles stun fishes and other animals on which the anemones

feed. Anemones cling to rocks and are frequently found in rock pools. They pull in their tentacles and shrink to a blob of jelly if they are left uncovered by the tide.

Sea beet A flowering plant of the goosefoot family, found around the coast. It is the wild ancestor of beetroot and sugar beet. It has long upright stems with tough leaves and tiny green flowers.

Sea cucumber A group of echinoderms, distantly related to the starfishes. These sausage-shaped, slow-moving animals have a mouth fringed with tentacles that are used for picking up food particles. When in danger, sea cucumbers can shoot out sticky threads to entangle their enemy, giving themselves time to crawl to safety.

Sea cucumber

Sea fir Like coral polyps and hydra, sea firs live in colonies. Another name for them is hydroids. They start life as free-swimming larvae which later settle on the sea bed and form colonies. The result looks like a many-branched coral, or indeed a fir tree.

Sea gooseberry Member of a group of marine animals called comb jellies. As their name implies, sea gooseberries look like gooseberries and have 'combs' of tiny hairs on the sides of their bodies. They are almost transparent and swim about in the sea by using their hairs as oars. They feed on other small animals.

Sea hare A group of molluscs named after their hare-like 'ears' (which are not ears at all). Sea hares are a form of sea slug. They are very well camouflaged and can also give off an inky 'smokescreen' to help them hide from an enemy.

Sea holly A flowering plant of the carrot family found by the coast. Sea holly is so called because it has prickly, waxy leaves similar to those of the holly. It also bears tightly-packed, rounded flowerheads which are greyish-blue in colour.

Sea kale A flowering seashore plant of the cabbage family. The stem is thick and bears clusters of white, four-petalled flowers. Ranged up the stem are large wrinkled leaves which look similar to cabbage leaves.

Sea-lettuce Also known as green laver, this is a green seaweed with wide, lettuce-like fronds.

Sea mat Also known as moss animals, these curious creatures form mats on rocks and seaweeds. They are mostly marine and live in colonies, each animal in its own horny cell, collecting food in its waving tentacles. One kind, the hornwrack, has branching frond-like colonies that look like seaweed.

Sea mouse A bristle worm which gets its name from its mouse-like way of moving, and from the hairy coat on its oval body. It lives in the sand below the low water mark. Sea mice grow to 18 cm long.

Sea potato This animal looks like a potato (hence the name), but it is actually a sea urchin. Its hard

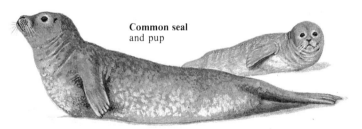

Common seal and pup

Seal A carnivore that is specialized for life in the sea. Its short legs form flippers that are good for swimming but useless on land, so the animal has to drag itself along the ground on its belly. A thick layer of blubber beneath the skin insulates seals from the cold. Two species of seal, the common and the grey, are found off NW Europe's coasts.

Sea lavender A group of flowering plants often found on the coast and in saltmarshes. The common sea lavender bears flat-topped clusters of lavender-coloured flowers. The leaves are borne on long stalks near the base of the stem.

skeleton or test may sometimes be found on the shore at low tide. The sea potato is a burrower; another name for it is the sand urchin.

Sea slater A crustacean similar to a wood-louse, which lives on the seashore. The commonest European slater is over 2 cm long and roams about the tide line, feeding on seaweed. Special sense organs in its legs warn it if a rock pool is too salty for it to live in.

Sea slug A form of sea snail that has either a very small shell or no shell at all. Sea slugs can crawl along the sea bed feeding on corals, sea anemones and other coelenterates. Their flattish bodies are covered with feathery bits of skin, which act as gills for breathing. Many sea slugs are brightly coloured and poisonous.

Sea snail (1) A group of gastropod molluscs which look much like land snails but which breathe with gills instead of lungs. They also have a horny disc, called an operculum, with which they close up their shells. Many are carnivorous; they bore through the shells of other molluscs with rasping tongues called radulae. Others browse on seaweeds. Examples of sea snails are the ORMER, TOPSHELL, WINKLE and WENTLE-TRAP. (2) The name given to two species of tiny fish from the Arctic Circle which visit northern coasts. Sea snails are only 15 cm long and are shaped like tadpoles. They have a long fin running along the back.

Gooseberry sea squirt

Sea squirt A group of marine animals usually found attached to rocks or underwater structures. Sea squirts feed by filtering floating matter from the water. They are TUNICATES. Examples of the 1200 or so species are the gooseberry, star and tube sea squirts. Some live singly, others live in groups or colonies.

Sea urchin A group of echinoderms, related to the starfishes. The animals are enclosed in a hard spiny case or test, made up of hundreds of chalky plates. Empty tests can often be found washed up on the shore. Sea

Sea urchin
and test

urchins have no arms, unlike starfishes, but they can move by means of tube-feet. They feed by browsing on seaweeds or by collecting debris from the sea bed. Some species have poisonous spines. The SEA POTATO is a sea urchin.

Seaweed A large group of marine algae found mostly around the shore. Seaweeds do not have leaves but fronds, many of which are leaf-like. The main part of the plant is called the frond. Seaweeds are anchored by a sucker-like organ called a holdfast. There are three basic types of seaweed: green, brown and red. Different kinds tend to be found in different zones on the beach. Red seaweeds are rarely found above the low tide mark as they cannot withstand conditions out of water. Brown seaweeds such as wracks may cover large rocky areas between the low and high tide marks. The green seaweeds which make the rocks slippery are usually found on the upper parts of the shore.

Sedge A large family of grass-like flowering plants, commonly found in grassy places and near water. The triangular stem bears long slender leaves and spikes of tiny male and female flowers.

Sedge fly See CADDIS FLY.

Seed The reproductive body of flowering plants and conifers. It consists of a miniature plant, the embryo, surrounded by a tough coat. The seed also contains a store of food which may be inside the embryo or packed around it. The embryo uses this stored food when it starts to grow (see GERMINATION).

Segment A compartment of an animal's body, repeated almost identically over its length.

Self-heal A small creeping plant related to the dead-nettle and commonly found in grassy places.

Self-heal

The stem of the plant is slightly hairy and bears a short spike of purple, two-lipped flowers. The plant spreads by means of underground shoots or rhizomes.

Sepal One of the outermost parts of a typical flower, usually green and leaf-like and surrounding the petals before they open. They sometimes fall as the flower opens, but usually simply bend back under the petals. Not all flowers have sepals, and sometimes the sepals are just like the petals.

Sequoia, giant A coniferous tree that grows wild in the Sierra Nevada of California. Though not as tall as the coast redwood to which it is related, In Europe, where it is grown as an ornament, the tree rarely exceeds 50 metres in height.

Serin A small finch of southern Europe that is gradually moving north-westward to breed. Its plumage is yellow with brown streaks. The bird nests in trees and

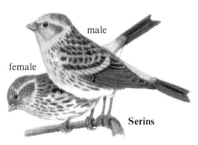

male

female

Serins

bushes and is often found in parks and wooded areas in towns.

Serpent star See BRITTLE STAR.

Service tree A small group of deciduous trees belonging to the rose family. The wild service tree has acidic-tasting, hawthorn-like leaves, small brown fruits and a flaky bark. The true service tree has compound leaves made up of 13 or more leaflets, rather like those of the rowan. Its small, pear-shaped fruits are sweet when ripe. The bastard service tree is a cross between the rowan and the whitebeam.

Set The cluster of burrows inhabited by a family of badgers.

Sexton beetle See BURYING BEETLE.

Shad A fish belonging to the herring family. There are two European species. The allis shad lives in estuaries, and migrates well inland to spawn. Its close relative the twaite shad spends its life further out to sea, but also migrates up river to spawn. Both fishes are about 40 cm long, with a number of black spots along the sides.

Shag A large bird of the sea coast, like the cormorant in appearance, but smaller and with no white patch on its face. The plumage is glossy green-black, and the bird has a small crest on its head during the breeding season. Shags dive to catch fish.

Shark A group of about 250 species of cartilaginous fish of which a dozen or so regularly visit European waters. Sharks have skeletons made of cartilage (gristle) instead of bone and most have torpedo-shaped bodies. The teeth are modified scales. Many sharks are ferocious predators feeding on a wide range of fishes. They range in size from about 70 cm to 15 metres long. Most of them are harmless to humans, and many are edible. See BASKING SHARK, BLUE SHARK, DOGFISH, MONKFISH, PORBEAGLE, SPUR-DOG, THRESHER and TOPE.

Shearwater Seabirds related to the fulmar. They are mostly black or brown above with white underparts. They feed on fishes, crustaceans and shellfish. The most common European species is the Manx shearwater.

Shelduck A large black and white bird, with green and chestnut markings. Shelducks live on sea coasts, feeding on seaweed and marine animals. The female nests in a burrow (usually a rabbit hole), often some distance from the sea.

Shell A hard coat, such as that of snails or other molluscs, made largely of lime. The hard coverings of crabs and other crustaceans are also called shells.

Shepherd's purse A common flowering plant of the cabbage family. It has small white flowers and gets its name from its heart-shaped seed-pods which are similar in shape to the purses worn by medieval shepherds. It is most commonly found on cultivated land.

Shepherd's purse

Shield bug See STINKBUG.

Shipworm A bivalve mollusc with a worm-like body. The best known shipworm is the teredo, which bores into wooden ships by using its two small shells as drills. The teredo makes a chalky tube to protect its soft body. It sucks in water and filters out any food particles in it.

Short-eared owl An owl with short ear tufts, more common than its relative the long-eared owl. The short-eared owl sometimes flies by day.

Shoveler A duck with a spade-like bill used to forage in the mud of ponds and marshes. The male is chestnut and white, with a dark green head, and a blue-black back. The female is brown. In winter, shovelers from northern Europe fly south to warmer feeding grounds.

Shrew A small insectivore, and the smallest of all the mammals. Shrews look like mice but have more pointed snouts and inconspicuous ears. The common shrew is the most abundant European species. It is about 7 cm long with a long tail and has sharp, red-tipped teeth. Active day and night in any well-vegetated habitat, it eats its own body weight in food every day. Its diet consists of

Common shrew

insects and other small creatures. See also PYGMY SHREW and WATER SHREW.

Shrike Birds commonly called butcher-birds because they store their food (smaller birds, mice and insects) by impaling it on thorns and spikes. They have hooked bills similar to those of birds of prey. The great grey shrike and the red-backed shrike are widespread in Europe, though the red-backed shrike is only a summer visitor.

Shrimp A group of marine crus-

Shrimp

taceans rather like tiny lobsters, and closely related to the prawns. Shrimps are an important food for many fishes and also for humans. Many shrimps are almost transparent. They eat a variety of smaller animals which they catch with their small pincers.

Shrub Any woody plant that habitually has several main stems or branches springing from, or very

near to, ground level.

Sickener, the A poisonous toadstool with a scarlet cap and pure white stalk. The gills are also pure white. It belongs to a group of fungi known as brittle gills and is found in coniferous woods in the autumn.

Silverfish A small wingless insect often seen running in baths and sinks. It belongs to a group of insects known as bristletails and has a three-pronged tail. The silverfish has bright silver scales. It eats practically anything, but does not do any

Silverfish

serious damage about the house.

Silverweed A flowering plant belonging to the rose family. Silverweed grows on waste ground and is a creeping plant with long runners, yellow flowers, silvery leaves and edible roots which were formerly dried and ground into flour.

Silver-Y A migratory moth with a silvery Y-shaped mark on each front wing. It flies by day and night, feeding on flowers. Large groups of silver-Y moths fly northwards across Europe in spring.

Siphon A muscular tube involved in the feeding and breathing of many aquatic molluscs.

Siskin A yellow finch that breeds in coniferous forests in most parts of Europe. The male is bright yellow and black; the female is browner. Siskins feed on the seeds of many kinds of trees. In winter they move to the south and west.

Skate, common The largest Atlantic ray, growing to a maximum length of 2.5 metres but usually smaller. It can be distinguished from the true

Skate

Grizzled skipper

Gatekeeper

Speckled wood and underside

Large skipper

Small skipper

Wall brown

Dingy skipper

rays by its dark belly: rays have white undersides. Adults have two rows of spines along the tail.

Skipper A family of butterflies named for their rapid, skipping flight. There are a number of species, including the grizzled skipper, dingy skipper, large skipper and chequered skipper. Most are an attractive mottled brown, and can be seen flying over grassland in the sunshine.

Skua Aggressive seabirds, renowned for their habit of chasing seagulls and other birds and forcing them to drop their prey, which the skuas then catch. The great skua and the Arctic skua occasionally visit the far

to form a naked mass of protoplasm that moves like an animal.

Sloe The fruit of the BLACKTHORN.

Slot The footprint of a deer. Each slot consists of two pointed impressions made by the toes and a narrow space between them. The pointed end is the front.

Slow worm A legless, shiny brown lizard found all over NW Europe except in the extreme north and Ireland. It is about 50 cm long including the tail and usually lives in damp places. As its name suggests it moves slowly, but it speeds up when danger threatens. It feeds largely on earthworms and slugs.

Slow worm

north of Scotland and Scandinavia to breed. They look similar to gulls but have brown plumage.

Skullcap Several species of flowering plant related to the dead-nettle. Skullcap is found in wet grassy areas and has two-lipped blue flowers which are borne in pairs at the base of the opposite-paired leaves.

Skylark A bird noted for its beautiful song, heard as the bird hovers in flight. Skylarks live in open meadowland and nest on the ground. They run rather than hop, and feed on insects and seeds. The skylark is a brownish bird, with pale underparts and a small head crest.

Slime mould Fungus-like organisms which, when growing, join together

Slug A group of gastropod molluscs, closely related to the snail but with only a tiny shell or no shell at all. Slugs are found in damp places, and usually come out to feed at night. Most kinds eat plants, but some slugs are carnivorous.

Smelt A slender member of the salmon family, only about 15 cm long. It lives close to the shore and in river estuaries, migrating inland to breed. Some smelts live permanently in freshwater lakes which formerly were linked with the sea.

Smooth newt One of Europe's most widespread newts, found over most of the north-west. It lives mainly on land, migrating in spring to the water to breed. It is mainly brown

Smooth newt

with an orange belly, and grows to about 11 cm long including the tail. In the breeding season the male becomes heavily spotted and develops a continuous wavy crest along its back and tail.

Smooth snake A dull-coloured snake, about 65 cm long. It is found over most of Europe except the far north, though it is very rare in Britain. It is slow-moving and non-poisonous, though it does bite.

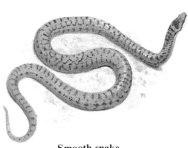

Smooth snake

Snail A group of gastropod molluscs found on land, in fresh water and in the sea. Some 50,000 species of snail are known. Most eat plants, but some eat other animals. The snail's shell protects it from enemies and also stops it from drying out. See GARDEN SNAIL, POND SNAIL, RAM'S HORN SNAIL and SEA SNAIL.

Snake Legless reptiles related to the lizards. Snakes have long slim bodies and tails, and scaly skins.

They cannot close their eyes. They move easily across rough ground either by looping their bodies sideways and pushing back against lumps in the surface, or by digging the broad scales on their bellies into the ground and pulling themselves forward. Snakes can eat prey far larger than themselves because the lower jaw is not connected to the skull. They swallow their prey whole. Some snakes kill their prey by squeezing (constricting) it to death; others have poisonous fangs. No snakes are found in Ireland. See ADDER, GRASS SNAKE, SMOOTH SNAKE, VIPERINE SNAKE and WHIP SNAKE.

Snake fly A group of insects with long 'necks' which they raise high above their bodies, resembling snakes poised to strike. They are related to alder flies. Snake flies live in woods. The female lays her eggs

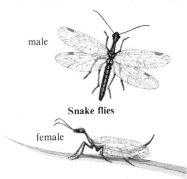

male

Snake flies

female

beneath the bark of trees by inserting her long ovipositor.

Snapdragon Flowering plants related to the figwort and toadflax. They have stalked spikes of two-lipped flowers. Unlike those of the similar toadflax, their flowers are not spurred; instead there is a small pouch for the nectar. The mouth of the flower is closed. The flowers vary in colour from reds and purples to yellow, and are widely cultivated. In the wild they grow in dry bare places.

Sneezewort A flowering plant of the daisy family. Sneezewort has thin, toothed leaves and loose clusters of white flowers. The flowers are made up of both disc and ray FLORETS. The plant is found in damp grassy places.

Snipe Wading birds of moorland and marshes, mottled brown with dark stripes on the head. Snipe fly in zigzags when alarmed. During courtship, the male performs a fast diving flight, vibrating his wings and tail to make a loud noise. This is called drumming. Snipe nest on the ground and feed on insects and worms.

Snowdrop A small plant with narrow, greyish, grooved leaves. The white, bell-shaped flowers have green-tipped inner petals; they flower very early. Found in damp, shady places.

Soapwort Sprawling plants related to the campions and pinks, usually found on waysides. The leaves of the soapwort excrete a lathery substance when rubbed vigorously in water. The pink, five-petalled flowers are borne in small clusters.

Social insect Any of those insects that live in an organized community – which is always a family unit – and co-operate with each other for the good of that community. All ants and termites are social insects, and so are many bees and wasps.

Sole A flatfish found mostly on

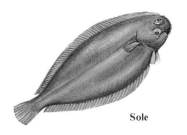

Sole

sandy or muddy sea beds around the coasts of Europe. Its range does not extend as far north as many of the other flatfishes. The fish is about 40 cm long. It buries itself in the sand by day and hunts at night.

Sorrel Flowering plants belonging to the dock family. The common sorrel has arrow-shaped leaves and thick whorls of small green and red flowers arranged in branched spikes. It is found in wooded areas and grassland.

Sow-thistle Several flowering plants belonging to the daisy family. Sow-thistles are widespread weeds of fields and wasteground. They have yellow or mauve dandelion-like flowers, and the toothed leaves are covered in spines.

Spadefoot toad A small toad, about 7 cm long, with a spade-like growth on its hind feet used for digging. The

Common spadefoot toad

pupils of its eyes are vertical, which readily distinguishes it from the common and most other toads. The common spadefoot occupies central Europe from France eastwards. It smells of garlic and screams when attacked, digging itself quickly into the sandy soil where it lives.

Sparrow Small streaky brown birds with pale underparts and stout seed-crushing beaks. Sparrows tend to live in large flocks. The two most common European species are the house and tree sparrow. The hedge sparrow is an unrelated species also known as the DUNNOCK.

Sparrowhawk

Sparrowhawk A bird of prey which hunts by patrolling the edges of woods and hedgerows, seizing any small bird, and occasionally mice, frogs and insects. The female's plumage is grey above and white beneath; the male is brick-red underneath, with darker bars.

Spawn (1) A mass of small eggs, especially of fishes and of frogs and toads. (2) The mycelium of mushrooms and toadstools.

Spearwort Flowering plants related to the buttercup. They grow in marshy places, and have long, spear-shaped leaves and yellow flowers. The greater spearwort's leaves grow up to 25 cm high, the lesser spearwort's up to 4 cm.

Species Any one kind of plant or animal. All the individuals in a species can interbreed to produce more of the came kind, but they cannot normally breed with another species.

Speckled wood A common brown butterfly which prefers shady woodland, where its speckled wings make it hard to see. It has orange to yellow markings on a dark brown surface.

The caterpillar is green and feeds on grasses.

Speedwell A group of flowering plants belonging to the same family as the foxglove, and found growing in woods, hedgerows and roadside banks. Most speedwells have creeping stems which root and send up straight stalks bearing heart-shaped leaves and spikes of small blue flowers. The germander and common field speedwell are two widespread species.

Spider A group of arachnids whose bodies are divided into two parts: the prosoma (front section), and the abdomen. The prosoma carries a pair of poisonous fangs at the front, plus a pair of sensory palps and four pairs of walking legs. Spiders have silk glands in their abdomens and many species spin webs in which to catch their prey. Those that spin the classic circular or orb-shaped webs are called orb spiders. They include the GARDEN SPIDERS. Others, such as the HOUSE SPIDER, spin untidy sheet webs. But not all spiders spin webs; the WOLF SPIDER catches its prey by chasing it. See also JUMPING SPIDER, MONEY SPIDER and WATER SPIDER.

Spider-hunting wasp A family of solitary wasps which paralyse spiders to provide a food store for their young. The female wasp attacks the spider with her sting and drags the paralysed victim to her nest. There she lays an egg beside it; when the egg hatches, the wasp larva feeds on the spider.

Spindle shank A tufted toadstool with a tough, grooved brown stalk that becomes very narrow at the base. It has a dark red-brown cap and grows at the bases of tree trunks in summer and autumn.

Spindle tree A deciduous tree or shrub found throughout Europe and growing to a height of 6 metres. In autumn it produces bright pink fruits which split open to reveal the orange seeds. The pointed leaves turn red in autumn. The spindle tree's hard wood was once used for making spindles.

Spiny dog fish See SPUR DOG.

Spiracle The opening of an insect's breathing tubes.

Spire shell Molluscs with spiral shells, including the WENTLETRAP; they live below the low tide mark.

Spitting spider See HOUSE SPIDER.

Spittle bug See FROGHOPPER.

Sponge A group of simple animals found mainly in warm, shallow seas. Most sponges look like plants but are in fact made up of colonies of tiny animals with sandy or chalky skeletons.

Spoonbill A large white wading bird similar to storks, with long legs and a long flattened bill which ends in a spoon-like tip. The spoonbill uses its bill to hunt for small water creatures. Spoonbills are usually found in swamps and other wet places.

Spore A minute reproductive body that is released by flowerless plants and which gives rise, directly or indirectly, to a new individual.

Spotted woodpecker Three species of woodpecker, of which the largest

Great
spotted
woodpecker

and most common is the great spotted or pied woodpecker. They are essentially black and white birds with red markings. The pied woodpecker often drums on wood, and rarely feeds on the ground. The lesser spotted or barred woodpecker is much the smallest of the woodpeckers and drums faster than the others, though not so loudly. Unlike the other two, the middle spotted woodpecker is not found in Scandinavia or the British Isles.

Spring beauty A short flowering plant belonging to the purslane family. The spring beauty has five-petalled white flowers, one pair of pointed oval leaves encircling each flowering stem. It likes sandy soils.

Springtail A group of primitive wingless insects which get their name from the forked 'spring' at the rear of the body. They can flick this spring downwards and thrust themselves into the air if disturbed. Springtails live mainly among the dead leaves beneath trees.

Springtail

Spruce Member of a group of about 40 coniferous trees belonging to the pine family. The Norway spruce is the traditional Christmas tree. It is native to northern and central Europe, and is widely grown for its timber. It reaches a height of 40 metres and has sharp-pointed, four-sided needles and long drooping cones. The sitka or silver spruce comes from western North America. It grows very fast up to 50 metres tall in Europe. Its needles are flatter and sharper than those of the Norway spruce, and its bark tends to flake

Norway spruce

off. It produces soft timber called whitewood.

Spur-dog A small shark that rarely grows over one metre, and has a sharp spine in front of each dorsal fin.

Spurge A large group of flowering plants whose stems contain a poisonous milky juice. The reproductive organs of the flower are borne, without petals or sepals, inside a small green 'cup' formed by the bract. The flowers are arranged in loose clusters and the undivided leaves grow alternately up the stem.

The various species grow in a wide range of habitats.

Spurrey Several flowering plants related to the pinks and campions. They have whorls of long thin leaves ranged along the stem and small, star-shaped, five-petalled flowers. The white-flowered corn spurrey is a common weed of cultivated land. The sea spurreys have pink flowers; they are found in saltmarshes and on coastal rocks.

Squid A group of marine cephalopod molluscs, related to the octopus and cuttlefish. Squids have eight arms and two long tentacles used to seize prey. They swim rapidly by squirting out jets of water from a siphon tube, and can also hide themselves by giving off a cloud of inky liquid. The largest squids can be 18 metres long, including the tentacles.

Squill Plants closely related to the bluebell with attractive blue star-shaped flowers and long, grass-like leaves. The plants are found in grassy places, often near the sea.

Squirrel Three types of rodent are called squirrels: tree squirrels, of which two species are found in

Grey squirrel

Europe; flying squirrels; and ground squirrels such as the MARMOT. The two European tree squirrels are the red and the grey. They have long bushy tails and sharp claws that help them when climbing. Both are active by day. The red squirrel is native to Europe. It is about 25 cm long and has distinctive long hairy ear tufts during the winter. It eats mainly conifer seeds. The slightly larger grey squirrel was introduced to Britain from North America in 1876, since when it has spread rapidly, largely replacing the red squirrel in most parts of the country. Its favourite food is acorns. The only flying squirrel in Europe lives in the forests of Finland and Russia. It is nocturnal.

Stag The male of the red deer and of some other kinds of deer.

Stag beetle A large beetle, up to 75 mm, with antler-like 'horns'. Only the males have horns, which are in fact over-developed mandibles or jaws. Despite their formidable appearance, stag beetles are harmless, though the female (which is smaller than the male) can give a painful nip if handled. Stag beetles

feed on sap, and are found mainly in oak woods. They fly at dusk and are often attracted by lights.

Stamen The male part of the flower, which produces the pollen. It consists of a slender stalk or filament and a hollow anther where the pollen grains are formed. There are often many stamens in one flower and they can produce millions of pollen grains.

Starfish Named after their star shape, these marine creatures are not fishes at all but echinoderms. They have a series of arms radiating from a central body. Many species have five arms but some have as many as 50. They use the TUBE-FEET on the undersides of their arms to pull apart the shells of oysters and other shellfish on which they feed. If an arm is broken off, the stump can regrow to full size.

Starling A common European bird which forms huge, noisy flocks in the autumn and winter months. At a distance starlings appear black, but their feathers actually gleam with specks of purple and green. On the ground they are easily distinguished because they walk, whereas other

female

male

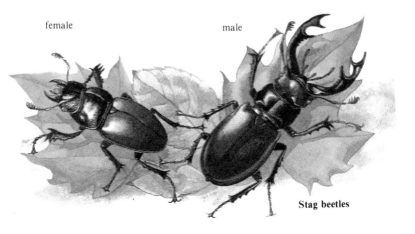

Stag beetles

Starlings

Male
in summer

Young
male

Male
in winter

songbirds hop. In the past hundred years starlings have taken to living in cities. They eat vast quantities of insects and are particularly fond of cherries. Starlings are good mimics of other birds, including thrushes and blackbirds.

Star of Bethlehem Several species of flowering plant belonging to the lily family. The common star of Bethlehem is found in grassy and cultivated places and bears delicate white, star-like flowers which can be recognized by the green stripe on the underside of each petal. Its leaves are grass-like.

Stem That part of a plant which bears the leaves and flowers. It contains lots of slender tubes carrying water and food between the leaves and the roots.

Stick insect These insects have long, slim bodies which look like twigs, so

that they are hidden from predators. They feed on leaves. The female of the species shown here can lay eggs which hatch without fertilization.

Stickleback Member of a group of fishes named for the spines on their backs. The nine-spined stickleback is found almost entirely in weedy ponds and brooks, though it also ventures into brackish water. Up to 7 cm long, it may have between seven and twelve spines on its back. The fifteen-spined stickleback is also called the sea stickleback, and is found only in inshore waters and river estuaries. It is very slender and

**Stick
insect**

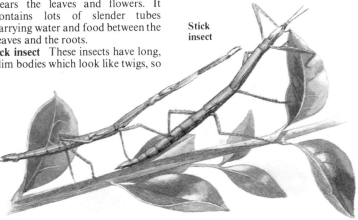

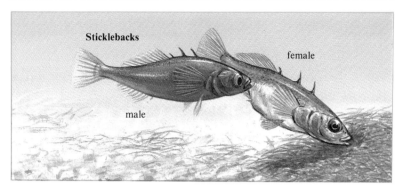

Sticklebacks

female

male

grows up to 20 cm long. The three-spined stickleback is about the same size as the fifteen-spined. It is found in both marine and freshwater habitats, the marine varieties returning to fresh water to spawn. Sticklebacks are nest-builders. The male builds a nest and guards the young fish when they hatch.

Stigma That part of the surface of the carpel of a flower that receives the pollen during pollination. It is sometimes raised up on a stalk known as the style.

Stinkbug Also called shieldbugs because of their shield-like shape, these insects look rather like beetles but are in fact true bugs. Their forewings form a hard shield over the delicate hind wings which are used for flying. Stinkbugs give off a foul-smelling fluid when disturbed. They feed by sucking sap from plants.

Stink fly See LACEWING.

Stinkhorn A woodland fungus that starts as a small 'egg' which grows to about the size of a golf ball and then splits open. A spongy stalk grows up from the 'egg'. Its cap is covered with foul-smelling, brownish slime containing millions of spores. A stinkhorn can be smelt long before it is seen.

Stitchwort A number of flowering plants belonging to the pink family. A common species is the straggling and widespread greater stitchwort. It has white, star-shaped flowers and narrow leaves. The plants were once thought to cure the muscular pain known as the stitch.

Stoat A small carnivore related to the weasel and found all over NW Europe. It is about 27 cm long with a long tail and short legs. The summer coat is brown, and the winter coat in northern regions is pure white

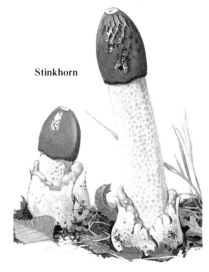

Stinkhorn

Stoats

summer
coat

winter
coat

except for a black tip to the tail. Further south, e.g. in southern England, the winter coat is brown, sometimes with white patches. The pure white varieties are called ermine and are much prized for their fur. Stoats prey on mice, voles and occasionally rabbits, often hunting by day. They have musk glands at the base of the tail and can give off a strong smell when frightened.

Stock dove A dove which takes its name from the old meaning of the word 'stock', a tree-stump. The birds nest in such stumps, or in holes in banks and buildings. They look like wood pigeons, but have narrower wings and tails and no white markings. They like open parklands.

Stonechat A small bird related to the thrush, usually living on heathland or similar open country. It is a chestnut colour, with white bars on its wings, and the male has a black head with a white collar. It feeds on insects and grubs, and usually nests low down in bushes. Stonechats have a jerky flight, and a call like two stones being banged together.

Stonecrop A family of flowering plants common in dry rocky places; many are creeping evergreens. Stonecrops have fleshy leaves and stems, and bear small star-shaped pink, yellow or white flowers which are usually borne in flat-topped clusters.

Stonefly A group of dull-coloured insects of the river bank, which have long, slender bodies with overlapping wings. The stonefly nymph has two whip-like tails at the rear of its body. It lurks on the river bottom, feeding on plants and small water animals.

Stonewort A group of branched green algae that bear a resemblance to higher plants. They have whorls of thin branches and are normally found in lakes and ponds. Stoneworts become encrusted with lime which makes them brittle and earns them their name.

Stork A group of large birds with long legs and a long neck. They look ungainly in flight, with their necks outstretched and their legs trailing behind them. On the ground they have a slow, graceful gait. Two kinds of storks are found in Europe. Both are summer visitors from Africa, although they rarely visit Britain. White storks commonly nest on buildings, particularly chimneys. The black stork lives in marshes and builds its nest in trees. It breeds mainly in eastern Europe.

Storksbill Plants of the geranium family, with a long, twisted beak for fruit; found on bare ground by the sea.

Stormcock See THRUSH.

Storm petrel The smallest European seabird, usually found in the open ocean, often flying in the wake of a ship. It is a sooty-brown bird with a white band across its tail. The petrel comes ashore only to breed, laying its single egg on clifftops or rocky ledges. It feeds on shellfish, fishes and other small sea creatures.

Stridulation The production of sound by rubbing one part of the body against another.

Sturgeon

Sturgeon A survivor of a prehistoric group of fishes, which has armour made up of bony plates. It lives at sea but travels up rivers to spawn in fresh water. It grows about 4 metres long but most individuals are smaller. Eggs from the female form caviar, a great delicacy. Sturgeons are now very rare in western Europe.

Style See STIGMA.

Succession The progressive changes seen in a habitat as the vegetation strives to gain or regain its natural state. The natural vegetation of most parts of Europe is woodland; the climate favours the growth of trees, so that most areas, left alone, will eventually become wooded.

Sulphur tuft A woodland toadstool that grows in clumps on the bases of tree stumps. It is very common, especially in autumn. The cap is sulphur-yellow. The gills are also yellow at first; later they turn olive-green.

Sulphur tuft

Sundew A group of insect-eating, flowering plants found in bogs and wet moors. They have a basal rosette of long-stalked, reddish leaves and tall, leafless stems bearing a spike of small white flowers. The leaves are covered in long sticky hairs which are stimulated when an insect lands on them, causing the leaf to curl inwards. In this way the insect becomes trapped, and can then be digested by the plant.

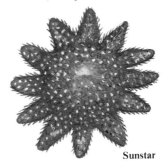

Sunstar

Sunstar A starfish that lives on rocks at low tide level. The common sunstar has 12 stubby arms and looks like a child's drawing of the sun.

Swallow A graceful, streamlined bird whose arrival in Europe every spring is generally seen as heralding the summer. It has blue-black upper parts with a red throat and white underparts. Although often confused with swifts and martins, swallows can be readily identified by the two long streamers on their forked tails. The birds spend much of their time on the wing, catching

167

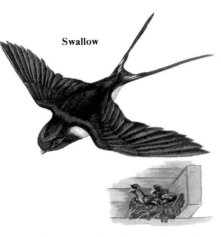

Swallow

hind wings. It is most often seen on summer flowers, especially in warm countries where there may be two or three broods in a summer. It is very rare in Britain, restricted to the Norfolk Broads.

Swallow-tailed moth A pale-coloured moth with pointed 'tails' on its rear wings. In flight, it floats in a ghostly manner along hedgerows and in gardens. The larva is camouflaged to look like a twig, remaining motionless during the day.

Swan Large water birds, belonging to the duck family, with elegant long necks. Swans are powerful birds and strong fliers. They have webbed feet for swimming and feed on water plants and animals. The common mute swan and the rarer Bewick's and whooper swans are white. The black swan of Australia is a popular ornamental species. Mute swans are also often seen in parks and water gardens. Pairs mate for life and guard their young, or cygnets, with great care.

insects, and rarely land on the ground, preferring to perch on telegraph wires or buildings. They build their nests on, or preferably in, buildings.

Swallowtail One of the most beautiful of European butterflies, with black and yellow markings and distinctive 'tails' trailing from its

Sweet chestnut A deciduous tree belonging to the beech family, also known as the Spanish chestnut. It grows best on dry sandy soils. The fruit consists of a spiky husk containing two or three shiny brown

Swallow-tailed moth

Swallowtail butterfly

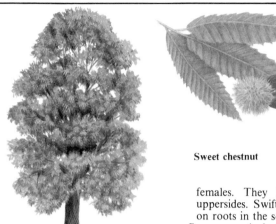

Sweet chestnut

nuts that are commonly eaten. The leaves are long and toothed. The tree is unrelated to the horse chestnut, even though it bears similar fruits.

Swift Fast-flying, streamlined birds which catch insects on the wing. They look and behave somewhat like swallows and martins but are unrelated. The common swift has dark brown plumage with a white throat, sickle-shaped wings and a forked tail. It winters in southern Africa and visits Europe from April to October. Swifts are among the fastest fliers of all birds. They are almost constantly in flight, eating and even sleeping on the wing. They have weak legs and land on the ground only by accident; they nest in high holes.

Swift moth A group of moths named for their fast flight and often seen flying around lights on summer evenings. Swift moths have small antennae. The two sets of wings are roughly the same shape, often brownish in colour with white markings. The males of the ghost swift are large moths which 'dance' over long grass to attract the females. They have pure white uppersides. Swift moth larvae feed on roots in the soil.

Sycamore A deciduous tree, native to southern and central Europe but now widely distributed further north. It belongs to the maple family and grows up to 35 metres tall. The bark is smooth and grey when young but becomes scaly as it gets older. The fruits consist of two winged seeds joined together.

Sycamore

Symbiosis An association between two organisms which is of benefit to both.

169

T

Tadpole The fish-like young of frogs, toads or newts. A tadpole has no leg at first, and swims by waving its tail. Legs gradually develop and the tadpole turns into the adult form and leaves the water. At the same time the animal must change from breathing with gills to breathing air with its lungs.

Tamarisk A tall, evergreen flowering shrub with tiny, scale-like leaves and stalked spikes of pink flowers. It is often planted by the sea to provide a windbreak.

Tansy A strong-smelling flowering plant of the daisy family. It bears clusters of yellow flowers made up of disc florets only. The leaves are divided into toothed leaflets and resemble the fronds of a fern. The plant grows on grassy waste ground.

Tapeworm A group of parasitic worms which live in the gut of many animals, including humans.

Tawny owl The deep 'hoo-hoo-hoo-oo' call of the tawny owl is the most familiar of the owl cries. The bird

Tawny owl

also has an uncanny 'e-wick' call. It is one of the most widespread and common owls, frequently found in towns.

Teal Small duck with several species found worldwide. The common teal is the smallest European duck. It lives on lakes and ponds, often moving away from the water to breed. The male has grey upper parts, and a chestnut head with a distinctive glossy green streak through the eye. The female is brown. As well as quacking, teal also make a whistling call.

Teasel A tall flowering plant with prickly stems and leaves. The tiny mauve flowers are tightly packed into a large conical head. When the flowers die they leave behind a head of hooked bracts. These spiky heads were once used for combing wool. Teasels usually grow in bare, often damp ground. Their dead stems and head usually remain standing throughout the winter.

Tellin Several species of burrowing bivalve mollusc common on the seashore. Tellins may lie up to 15 cm beneath the sand, feeding on tiny animals and debris on the sea bed through a siphon tube.

Tench A freshwater fish belonging to the carp family. It is usually a rich olive colour on top and lighter underneath, but its colouring varies with the surroundings in which it lives. Tench live among vegetation at the bottom of still and slow-moving water, feeding on insect larvae and other small animal life. In winter they hibernate in the mud.

Tendril Thread-like part of a stem or leaf which many climbing plants use to cling to their supports.

Teredo See SHIPWORM.

Tern Seabirds also known as sea swallows because of their pointed wings and forked tails. Terns are smaller than gulls, mostly white or grey, with dark heads. They nest in large colonies on rocks or sand dunes. Most often found is the common tern; other terns include the Sandwich tern, little tern and Arctic tern (which makes very long migratory flights).

European pond terrapin

Terrapin Mostly aquatic reptile closely related to the tortoise, but distinguished from it by its flatter shell and webbed toes. It always lives in or near water, eating fishes, frogs and other small pond creatures. During the winter it hibernates in the mud. The European pond terrapin is a common species found over most of central and southern Europe. It is about 20 cm long.

Territory An area adopted by an animal or a family or colony of animals as their home.

Test (1) A hard shell. (2) A seed-case.

Thistle A large group of flowering plants belonging to the daisy family. Most thistles have very spiny stems and leaves. Their composite flower-heads are made up of disc florets only, and they are usually purple and brush-like. The flowers are surrounded by usually spine-tipped,

sepal-like bracts. Many species are tall and erect, but the stemless thistle grows at ground level. Thistles are usually found in grassy or waste places.

Thorax (1) The middle of the three parts of an insect's body, carrying the legs and wings. (2) The upper part of the trunk in air-breathing vertebrates.

Thorn-apple A tall flowering plant related to the nightshades. It is a poisonous plant which gets its name from its spiny egg-shaped fruits. The thorn-apple has irregularly toothed, pointed leaves and large white trumpet-shaped flowers. It is often found on wasteland.

Thresher A shark that earns its name by its habit of scaring smaller fishes into a huddle by swimming round them threshing the water with its tail. It grows up to 6 metres in length and has a distinctively long upper section to its tail fin. It feeds mostly on shoaling fishes such as herring and mackerel.

Thrift A cushion-forming, flowering plant related to the sea lavender. It is often found near the coast and bears rounded heads of delicate pink flowers. The long narrow leaves grow around the base of the plant's otherwise leafless stems.

Thrips Small slender insects with narrow wings, often seen in summer on flowers. The forewings are characteristically fringed with long hairs, although some species are wingless. In winter, thrips hide away in cracks and crevices inside houses. They feed by sucking the juices of plants, and can be pests.

Thrush Common garden birds related to blackbirds and robins. The two most common European species are the song thrush and the mistle thrush. Both have brown upper parts and spotted breasts. The mistle thrush is the larger bird, with bōlder spots on its breast. Its habit of singing in bad weather when other birds are silent has earned it the nickname of stormcock.

Thyme, wild A mat-forming aromatic undershrub, with runners; found in grassy and healthy places.

Tick A group of tiny animals related to mites and spiders. Mammals and birds may be infested with these parasites which suck their blood and also spread disease. Ticks lay their eggs on plants and the young larvae cling on to passing animals.

Tiger beetle A group of fast-running, fast-flying beetles which hunt other insects. The larva lies in wait within a burrow, only its jaws sticking up above ground to seize any passing prey. The green tiger beetle is the most common species. It is bright green, with pale spots, and prefers sandy places.

Tiger moth A number of brightly coloured moths with dark blotches on their cream forewings, and red or orange hind wings. The striking pattern warns predators to leave the

Great tit

Blue tits

moth alone, for its taste is unpleasant and it has irritating hairs on its body. The tiger moth's hairy caterpillar is also known as the 'woolly bear'.

Timothy Several species of grass with long, sausage-shaped flower-heads. Some species have been cultivated for grazing cattle or hay making.

Tit A family of bright, perky little birds, also called titmice. Several of the world's 65 species are found in Europe, living in woodlands and frequenting gardens. Tits nest in holes in trees and eat mainly seeds and insects. They hunt together in large flocks after the breeding season and are acrobatic birds, readily hanging upside down from bags of nuts put out for them in gardens. See BLUE TIT, COAL TIT, GREAT TIT, LONG-TAILED TIT and MARSH TIT.

Titmouse See TIT.

Toad A tailless amphibian related to the frogs. In fact, both frogs and toads belong to the same group: animals with smooth skins are called

Coal tits

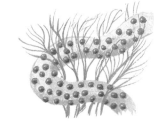

Common toad
with spawn and tadpoles

frogs, while those with rough skins are called toads. For the life cycle see FROG. The common toad is found all over NW Europe except Ireland. Up to 15 cm long, it is the largest European toad. The females are larger than the males. Common toads live in fairly dry places, hiding by day and feeding at night on slugs and other small animals. When alarmed they inflate their bodies to make them look bigger. See also MIDWIFE TOAD, NATTERJACK TOAD, SPADEFOOT TOAD and YELLOW-BELLIED TOAD.

Toadflax A number of flowering plants related to the figwort and snapdragon. They have narrow untoothed leaves and long leafy spikes of two-lipped flowers. The flowers may be yellow or varying shades of violet. They have long spurs which bear the nectar, and the mouth is always closed. Most species are found in bare or waste places.

Toadstool A term normally used for all those fungi with umbrella-shaped fruiting bodies.

Tope A small shark that grows up to 2 metres long. It lives close to the sea bed and feeds on bottom-living fishes.

Topshell A gastropod mollusc that gets its name because its cone-shaped shell looks like a child's spinning-top. It lives on the seashore and sea bed and is found only where the water is clean. Many live on rocks but others burrow into the sand.

Tormentil A creeping, mat-forming plant of the rose family, which bears loose heads of yellow, four-petalled flowers. It belongs to a group of plants called cinquefoils and is found on moors and grassland.

Tortoiseshell Two species of butterfly related to the peacock. Their uppersides are largely orange with dark markings, while the lower surfaces are dark brown. The small tortoiseshell is very common in gardens. Its spiky caterpillars feed in colonies on stinging nettles. The large tortoiseshell is much rarer, especially in Britain, and its caterpillars feed on elms, willows and other trees. Both species hibernate as adults. See picture on page 30.

Touch-me-not See BALSAM.

Tower shell A sea snail which spends most of its time partly buried in the sand below the low tide level. Its long spiral shell resembles a tower.

Transpiration The evaporation of water from a plant by way of tiny pores or stomata on the underside of the leaves.

Tree A large woody plant with just one main trunk.

Treecreeper Small birds with white bellies, and brown backs to blend with the trees on which they live. They feed almost entirely on insects which live in tree bark. Treecreepers run up, but not down, tree trunks. Two species are found in Europe. The short-toed treecreeper has a longer beak and shorter claws than the common treecreeper.

Tree frog A small, bright green frog, capable of climbing trees and bushes in search of insects to eat. It leaps into the air to catch flies on the wing. Tree frogs are only 5 cm long, with a dark stripe down either side of the body. They have little suction pads on their toes to give them grip while climbing. The frogs are found over most of southern and central Europe.

Tree of Heaven A deciduous tree that comes from China, and thrives in smoky, polluted atmospheres. It reaches a height of 18 metres and produces many upward-growing branches that form a tall crown.

Tree wasp Two species of wasp whose egg-shaped nests can be seen hanging from the branches of trees. The wasps make the nest from paper, chewing fragments of wood mixed with their own saliva to make a pulp that hardens as it dries. The nests are large, occasionally even up to 30 cm across. Tree wasps look very like common wasps.

Trefoil Several species of flowering plant belonging to the pea family. Their yellow, pea-like flowers are borne in small clusters of up to 30 flowers. The leaves of most species have trefoil leaves, i.e. leaves made up of three small leaflets. But some species, such as the common birdsfoot trefoil, have leaves made up of five leaflets, two of which are bent back so that there only appear to be three. Most trefoils grow in grassy places.

Tropism A bending movement of a plant in response to a directional stimulus. The bending of a stem towards light is a familiar example.

Trough shell A marine bivalve mollusc which burrows into sand below the low tide mark. It has a smooth cream-coloured shell and siphon tubes that reach out of the burrow. The trough shell can dig with surprising speed when alarmed.

Trout Member of a group of fast-swimming fishes closely related to the salmon and very similar in appearance. There are a great many varieties which differ mainly in their habits and colouring. Sea trout live part of their lives in the sea and part in fresh water. Other trout live all their lives in fresh water. The brown trout lives in rivers, whereas the lake trout spawns in rivers and then swims downstream to the lakes. The rainbow trout has been introduced from North America. Most species grow up to 1.4 metres long.

Tree of Heaven

Truffle Member of a group of edible fungi that have underground fruiting bodies shaped like potatoes.

Tube foot Any of the numerous little water-filled tubes projecting from the bodies of starfishes and related animals. Tube feet usually have a sucker on the end and they help the animals to move about or pull open mollusc shells.

Tubenose An order of ocean birds with external tubular nostrils above their hooked beaks. Includes STORM PETRELS, albatrosses, FULMARS and SHEARWATERS.

Tuber A swollen part of a root or underground stem, full of stored food and able to grow into a new plant when detached from the parent.

Tufted duck The commonest bay duck; the long tuft and black back of the drake are easily recognizable.

Tulip tree A tall, deciduous tree from North America belonging to the magnolia family and reaching a height of 35 metres. Its flowers are

Tulip tree

tulip-like, in shades from deep orange to pale green, but are often hidden amongst the angular and sometimes almost square leaves. A similar tree, the Chinese tulip tree, is also grown in Europe.

Tuna fish See TUNNY.

Tunicate Any member of a large group of marine animals including the sea squirts. Most are little more than soft, shapeless bags, pumping water into their bodies and filtering food from it before squirting it out again. The outer covering of the body is made from a translucent material called tunicin. Young tunicates look rather like tadpoles and drift in the plankton.

Tunny A large marine fish, also known as the tuna fish. Around Europe it is most common in the Atlantic, west of Spain, and in the Mediterranean, but after breeding it frequently migrates into northern waters in search of food. It grows up to 2 metres long and has a series of very small fins just in front of the tail. Tunny feed mainly on herring, mackerel and garfish.

Turbot A large flatfish, up to 60 cm long, that has bony platelets on its upper side. It is found on sandy or rocky sea beds and preys largely on other fish.

Turnstone A small wading bird of the seashore, which turns over pebbles to find food. Brown above and white beneath, the turnstone has a black patch on its breast, orange legs and a short bill.

Turtle dove The turtle dove earned its name by its sleepy call, 'tur-tur', which is the Latin for turtle. It is a summer visitor to Europe, avoiding the northern parts of the British Isles. It nests lower than other pigeons, usually in thick bushes.

Tusk shell A burrowing marine mollusc whose shell looks like a tiny elephant's tusk. Tusk shells can live at great depths on the sea bed. They use hair-like tentacles to collect food particles and small creatures from the mud.

Tussock moth A family of moths that get their name from the tufts of hairs on the caterpillars. Even the adults are hairy. The sharp points of these hairs cause irritation – especially to the throat of a predatory bird. Only cuckoos can eat tussock moths and their larvae. The family includes the VAPOURER and the GYPSY MOTH.

Twayblade Flowering plants belonging to the orchid family. The common twayblade, a plant of woods and grasslands, has yellow-green flowers on a long spike, emerging from two broad leaves. The lesser twayblade has pinkish flowers and is found on moors and bogs.

Twite A bird of the finch group, closely related to the linnet. Its name comes from the sound of one of its calls. Twites are small, brown-speckled birds which prefer moorland. They are seed-eaters and nest either on the ground or in low bushes.

Twite

U

Umbel A type of flowerhead characteristic of the carrot family. It is shaped rather like an umbrella, with all the individual flower stalks leaving the main stem at one point. The individual flowers are rather small, but there are so many packed into one umbel that the whole flowerhead is very conspicuous. Hogweed flowers, for example, grow in umbels.

Red underwing

Large yellow underwing

Underwing A group of moths with brownish or greyish upper wings and bright yellow or red underwings. To evade a hungry bird, the moth 'flashes' its underwings, then conceals them beneath the dull upper wings – so that it appears to vanish altogether. This disappearing trick is an example of 'flash coloration'.

Ungulate An animal whose toes end in hoofs – hard, horny growths.

V

Valerian A small group of hairless plants with thick clusters of usually pink flowers. The common valerian is found in woods and grassy areas, whereas the (greyish) red valerian prefers more rocky areas, on cliffs or in quarries. The roots of some species are eaten as a vegetable.

Valve One half of a bivalve shell, as found on mussels and clams.

Vapourer moth
with caterpillar
and wingless female

Vapourer moth A brown-winged tussock moth with two pale 'eye' spots. Only the male has wings; the wingless female spends her life close to the cocoon from which she emerged, even laying her eggs on it. The caterpillar has prominent tufts of dark and pale hairs. It feeds on many trees and shrubs.

Vector An animal that carries viruses and other disease-causing germs from one plant or animal to another.

Velvet shank A toadstool that gets its name from its velvety brown stalk. The tan-coloured cap is rather slimy and the gills are yellow and well separated. The fungus grows in large tufts on the stumps and fallen trunks of deciduous trees.

Vertebrate Any animal with a backbone. Fishes, amphibians, reptiles, birds and mammals are all vertebrates.

Vetch A number of mostly climbing, flowering plants belonging to the pea family, and usually found clambering in woods and hedges, or over grassland. They have mostly purple or lilac pea-like flowers, usually in stalked heads. Their leaves, which are divided into opposite-paired leaflets, end in long tendrils that help the plants to climb.

Vetchling Flowering plants of the pea family, with pink or yellow flowers, and (usually) tendrils branching off from the straggling stems.

Meadow vetchling

Violet Flowering plants related to the pansies, with heart-shaped leaves and delicate mauve or white flowers. Most violets like shady places, with plenty of moisture. There are a number of species, including dog violets, meadow violets, marsh violets and wood violets.

Viper See ADDER.

Viperine snake A harmless relative of the grass snake that gets its name because it looks rather like a viper. It reaches about 1 metre in length and feeds largely on fishes and amphi-

Viperine snake

bians. Viperine snakes are not found in Britain.

Virus One of many very tiny micro-organisms which can grow and multiply only inside the cells of plants and animals. All known viruses cause diseases.

Viviparous lizard A common brown lizard that gives birth to live young instead of laying eggs. It is found over most of Europe except the extreme south, and is Ireland's only reptile. It is about 17 cm long including the tail and lives in a variety of grassy places, both wet and dry.

Vole A small rodent closely related to the lemmings. Voles look similar to mice but have much shorter tails and smaller ears. They live mainly in grasslands and do not hibernate. The common vole is found over most of Europe except Britain and Scandinavia and digs shallow burrows. It measures 11 cm in length and is most active at dusk. See also FIELD VOLE, PINE VOLE and WATER VOLE.

Common vole

Wagtail Ground-living birds which walk and run about in a brisk jerky manner, wagging their long tails up and down. They eat insects and build their nests in holes, using holes in old buildings as well as those in rocks. The pied wagtail of Britain and the white wagtail of the Continent are familiar birds, varieties of the same species. Both are black, grey and white, but the pied wagtail is darker in the summer. They are commonly found near buildings, though the white wagtail also likes to be near water. Grey and yellow wagtails also prefer to live near water. Both are yellow birds but the grey wagtail is easily distinguished by its grey back and the black throat of the male.

Wall lizard A lizard commonly found in dry places in southern and central Europe, frequently near houses. It is about 20 cm long including the tail, and is usually brown with black spots. It is a good climber. See picture on page 109.

Walnut

Walnut A group of 15 species of deciduous tree with large, compound leaves. The most frequently grown is the common or English walnut. Originating in Asia and south-western Europe, the English walnut grows to a height of 30 metres. Its seeds are rich in oil.

Warbler A family of small insect-eating birds, many of which are good singers. Some are only distinguished by their song and behaviour. See BLACKCAP, CHIFFCHAFF, DARTFORD WARBLER, FIRECREST, GARDEN WARBLER, GOLDCREST, REED WARBLER, WHITETHROAT, WILLOW WARBLER and WOOD WARBLER.

Warm-blooded Able to maintain the blood at a constant temperature. Only birds and mammals are warm-blooded.

Warning coloration Vivid colour markings which protect poisonous or unpleasant-tasting animals, because predators quickly learn to recognize and avoid them.

Warty newt See CRESTED NEWT.

Wasp

Wasp A group of insects related to ants and bees, often with striking black and yellow markings that warn other animals that they are not good to eat. Like ants, wasps tend to have narrow 'waists'. Some species are social, living in colonies and building elaborate nests with paper which they make by chewing up wood. Others are solitary. Wasps feed mainly on fruit juices and nectar but they feed their larvae on flesh. Some are parasites, laying their eggs on the bodies of other insects, paralysed by the wasp's sting. The common wasp is a social species that makes its nest in old mouseholes or similar places in the ground. Each colony is founded by a queen, and lasts for one summer only. Fertilized queens hibernate through the winter, emerging to found new nests in spring. The HORNET is Europe's largest wasp. See also DIGGER WASP, GALL WASP, MASON WASP, PAPER WASP, POTTER WASP, RUBY-TAILED WASP, SAND WASP, and SPIDER-HUNTING WASP.

Water beetle Several groups of beetles found in ponds and streams, where they feed on other animals or on algae and rotting plant matter. Many can fly from pond to pond but they spend most of their lives under water. They use their wing cases as air tanks and surface from time to time to take in fresh air. One of the largest is the GREAT DIVING BEETLE. The WHIRLIGIG is also a water beetle.

Water boatman A group of aquatic bugs found in ponds, usually in the debris at the bottom where they feed on rotting vegetation. They swim to and from the surface to obtain bubbles of air. The name water boatman is also sometimes used for the BACKSWIMMERS.

Water flea A group of small, transparent crustaceans, also commonly known by their Latin name, *Daphnia*. They swim jerkily by beating their unusually long antennae. Water fleas form a large part of the plankton in ponds and lakes and are important as the chief food of many fishes.

Water lily Aquatic flowering plants that are unrelated to the true lilies. Water lilies are found in slow-moving or stagnant water. Their roots lie in the mud at the bottom of the pond, but their broad leaves, borne on long stalks, mostly lie floating on the surface of the water. The white water lily has large, fragrant white flowers and even larger, almost circular leaves. The yellow water lily has oval leaves on the surface and some smaller, thin, submerged leaves. The yellow flowers are smaller than those of the white water lily.

Water-louse A small freshwater crustacean related to the woodlouse. It belongs to the group of animals called isopods, and is commonly found in weedy ponds and streams.

Water ousel See DIPPER.

Water rat See WATER VOLE.

Water scorpion This is not in fact a scorpion, but an insect which lives in ponds. It looks like a dead leaf, and preys on other pond creatures, grabbing them with its front legs. It breathes air through a tube that reaches up to the surface.

Water shrew One of the largest of the shrews, about 8.5 cm long, and the only one that is a good swimmer. It eats mainly aquatic insects and lives in a burrow in the river bank, often with an entrance just under water.

Water spider The only spider to spend its entire life under water. It collects air bubbles and carries them down to fill an underwater 'diving bell' made of silk. Inside the bell, the spider rears its young. Water spiders catch other pond animals for food.

Water stick insect An aquatic bug related to the water scorpion. It has a slender, stick-like body and, since its front legs are adapted into graspers for seizing prey, the insect appears to have only four legs (instead of six). It lives in shallow ponds and breathes through a long 'tail' or siphon which it pokes through the surface of the water.

Water vole A large vole found throughout NW Europe except Ireland. It is about the size of a rat

(20 cm long) and is sometimes called a water rat, although it has much smaller ears and a blunter snout than true rats. It lives on the banks of rivers and ponds and is a good swimmer. Its diet consists of corn, bark and other plant food.

Waterweed, Canadian A common aquatic plant found submerged in stagnant or slow-moving fresh water. The oblong dark green leaves grow in thick whorls. The small white flowers are borne on long stems and float on the surface of the water. Male and female flowers grow on separate plants.

Wattle, silver See MIMOSA.

Waxwing The only European representative of a small family of fruit-eating, tree-living birds. It breeds in the extreme north of Europe in coniferous and birch forests, and some birds move south to winter. Every few years there is a population explosion in the south. The bird has a distinctive crest, black chin, yellow-tipped black tail, and waxy red blobs on its wings.

Wayfaring tree A small deciduous tree or shrub, about 6 metres tall,

Water vole

Wayfaring tree

related to the elder. It gets its name because it grows along roadsides, as well as on the edge of woodlands. It has heart-shaped, dusty-looking leaves, clusters of small white flowers, and flattened oval fruits which turn red and then black.

Weasel Smallest of the carnivores, closely related to the stoat. It is only about 20 cm long with short legs, and has a shorter tail than its cousin, with no black tip. In many areas the coat is brown both winter and summer, but in the north of Scandinavia the winter coat is pure white. Weasels are found throughout Europe except Ireland. They hunt by day and night for mice and voles, sometimes climbing trees for birds and eggs. Like stoats, they have musk glands at the base of the tail and can give off a strong smell when in danger or marking a trail.

Weasel

Weed A plant growing (habitually) where it is not wanted, usually a wild plant growing in the garden.

Weever Either of two species of fish found in European coastal waters. The greater weever is up to 40 cm long, while the lesser weever is only 15 cm long. Both bury themselves in the sand by day, with just their eyes and mouths showing, waiting for prey. They have highly poisonous spines on their back.

Weevil A group of small beetles with pointed snouts, which infest stores of flour and other food. They also eat plants and some, such as the cotton boll weevil, are pests. More than 40,000 species are known, of which 500 are found in Europe. The nut weevil has a particularly long snout which it uses to bore into hazel nuts.

Wels See CATFISH.

Wentletrap A sea snail with a narrow, distinctly ridged, spiral shell. Its name comes from a Dutch word meaning a spiral staircase. The wentletrap's eggs look like a necklace strung on a string, one end of which is anchored in the sand.

Whale Several large aquatic mammals with flippers. They breathe through a blowhole on top of the head, and feed mainly on krill.

Wheatear A small bird belonging to the thrush family, found on moors, hills and cliffs. The wheatear is a grey and white bird with black wings, recognizable by the white flash of its rump as it flies in a jerky manner close to the ground. It feeds on insects and makes its nest in a hole such as a disused rabbit burrow.

Whelk Several species of sea snail which live on the sea bed below low tide level. Many whelks are found on sandy or muddy shores, as are their sponge-like egg cases.

Whinchat A member of the thrush

family, breeding in Europe on open heaths and bushy grassland. It often bobs its tail, of which the outer feathers have a white base (distinguishing it from the STONECHAT).

Whip snake, western A fast-moving snake commonly found in France and Italy. It is about 1.5 metres long and though it is not poisonous it bites hard. It enjoys dry, sunny places and feeds on a variety of lizards and other animals, including snakes.

Whirligig beetle A group of water beetles that live on the surface of ponds and streams. They get their name from their characteristic whirling or spinning motion.

Whiskered bat One of the most widely found bats in Europe. It is 4.5 cm long and is sometimes seen flying by day. It flies rather more slowly than most bats.

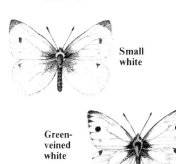

Small white

Green-veined white

White A group of predominantly white butterflies. The large and the small white are commonly called cabbage whites because they feed on plants of the cabbage family. Unlike most butterflies, the green-veined white flies on cloudy days.

White admiral A butterfly of European woodlands that often feeds on bramble flowers. Its black-and-white wings make the insect

White admiral and caterpillar

hard to spot on sun-dappled leaves. The white admiral caterpillar feeds on honeysuckle.

Whitebeam A deciduous tree, belonging to the rose family, that grows up to 25 metres tall. It likes chalky soil, and can withstand the pollution of city streets. It bears deep scarlet fruit and the lower surface of its leaves is covered with white hairs.

Whitefish Any of a group of slim silver fishes related to salmon and trout, mostly found in large lakes in Britain, the Alps and parts of Scandinavia. Some feed on plankton, while others hunt for their food at the bottom of the lakes. The powan, houting and vendace are among the best-known species.

Whitehound See TOPE.

Whitethroat A warbler found throughout most of Europe in the

Whitethroat

summer. It winters in Africa, where its numbers were greatly reduced by a drought in 1969. As its name implies, it has a conspicuous white throat; its plumage is otherwise greyish-brown. It lives on insects and ripe fruit. The lesser whitethroat is only slightly smaller than the common whitethroat, and is easily distinguished by its duller, greyer plumage and dark eye-patch.

Whiting A marine fish belonging to the cod group. There is a black spot at the base of the pectoral fin and no barbel on the mouth. Whiting are common around the coasts of Europe.

Whitlow grass This plant is not in fact a grass, but a member of the cabbage family. There are several species, found mostly on bare or rocky ground. The common whitlow grass bears stalked spikes of tiny white flowers.

Whorl (1) A group of leaves or flowers emerging from around the stem at one point. (2) A single turn in a spiral shell.

Wigeon A dabbling duck found on sea coasts, river estuaries and lakes. The male is grey and chestnut, with white underparts and yellow on the forehead. The female is a mottled brown all over. Wigeon feed on water plants, shellfish and insects.

Wild cat A carnivore that, at a glance, looks like a domestic tabby.

Wild cat

It is found in mountain forests of southern and central Europe, and in Scotland. It is about 60 cm long and has a thick bushy tail with dark rings around it. Like its domestic cousin, the wild cat is a solitary animal that prefers to hunt at night.

Willow A group of deciduous trees and shrubs, most of which have long, narrow leaves. Willows have single-sexed flowers arranged as catkins, male and female catkins occurring on different trees. Most species like damp soil. The white willow is one of the most common members of the group. It is a tall, pliant tree which grows up to 25 metres high, and is often found close to water. The goat willow or sallow gets its alternative name of pussy willow from its furry catkins. Shrub-like in shape, it grows to a height of 16 metres.

White willow

Willowherb A family of flowering plants, most of which have slender leaves that resemble those of a willow. The pinkish-purple, four-petalled flowers are borne in long spikes. The common rosebay willowherb prefers damp open woodland, and is often called fireweed because it quickly colonizes ground that has been burned.

Willow tit See MARSH TIT.

Willow warblers

Willow warbler A poorly named bird that has little to do with willows. It lives mostly in woods, feeding on insects. It builds its nest on the ground using dried grass and moss. The willow warbler has a greyish-green plumage and a quiet, tuneful song. It is abundant in northern Europe during the summer but migrates to Africa in autumn.

Windflower See ANEMONE.

Winkle Several species of small sea snail, also called periwinkles. Most winkles live in water, and breathe through gills. But some species live close to high tide level and are out of water for most of the time. They have lungs for breathing.

Wireworm The larva of certain CLICK BEETLES, disliked by gardeners because they damage the roots of plants.

Woad A flowering plant belonging to the cabbage family. It has arrow-shaped leaves and bears loose clusters of tiny yellow flowers. It is found on dry waste ground.

Wolf Although they prefer to hunt in packs in open country, European wolves are now furtive, nocturnal, forest hunters.

Wolf-fish A bottom-living fish found all round the western coasts of Europe. It grows up to 1 metre long and tapers strongly towards the tail. Wolf-fish have strong teeth to crush the shellfish on which they feed.

Wolfsbane A flowering plant of the buttercup family. It has divided leaves and bears spikes of yellow, hooded flowers. The plant is poisonous to humans and is found in shaded woodlands.

Wolf spider A group of spiders that hunt by running after their prey, usually insects. They do not spin webs. Most wolf spiders are small and dull coloured. The females carry their eggs around with them, inside silken white sacs attached to the rear of their abdomens.

Wolverine A carnivore belonging to the weasel family. It lives in Scandinavian forests and looks rather like a small bear. It is about 75 cm long with dark brown fur, and is sometimes called the glutton because it eats anything it can find, including carrion. It is even capable of killing reindeer.

Woodcock A wading bird rather like its smaller relative the snipe, with a long bill. The woodcock lives in damp woodland, and has handsome brown plumage, barred with black and chestnut. It uses its long bill to probe for worms.

Woodlark A bird similar in general appearance to its relative, the skylark. The woodlark is smaller, with a shorter tail and a more obvious crest on its head. It lives in open country, as well as in woodland, and like the skylark has a tuneful song.

Woodlouse The only crustaceans that live permanently on land. Woodlice are often found beneath stones or in damp places indoors. They are scavengers, feeding on rotting plant matter. Some woodlice can roll their armoured bodies into a ball for protection.

185

Wood mouse Also called the long-tailed field mouse, this mouse is found throughout Europe except in the extreme north. It is about 9.5 cm long and is the most abundant rodent, though it is rarely seen because it is nocturnal. It can run, jump and climb with ease and feeds mainly on seeds. The yellow-necked mouse, distinguished by a large yellow patch under its neck, and also somewhat brighter in colour, is a close relative. Both mice live in woods and gardens, and often enter houses.

Wood mouse

Wood mushroom A large woodland toadstool with a swollen, bulb-like base to the stalk and a droopy ring beneath the brownish gills. The ring is sometimes double. The cap and stalk become yellow with age.

Wood owl See TAWNY OWL.

Woodpecker A bird renowned for the rat-a-tat noise it makes while hammering into a tree trunk with its chisel-like bill. Only a few of the world's 179 species of woodpecker are found in Europe. The birds have strong feet, usually with two toes pointing forward and two backward, with which they can climb vertically up tree trunks. With their strong bills they can drill large holes into wood in search of insects or to make their nests. They generally attack trees that are rotten on the inside. The most widespread European woodpeckers are the GREEN WOODPECKER and the SPOTTED WOODPECKERS. The black woodpecker is found chiefly in Scandinavia and eastern Europe. It is the largest of the woodpeckers, and is totally black except for a red crown; the male also has a red crest.

Wood pigeon Also known as the ring dove, this is the largest European pigeon. It is a bird of the woodlands but is often found in city parks. Its five-note cooing is a familiar sound of the countryside. The parent bird secretes a substance in its crop on which the fledglings feed; this is known as 'pigeon milk'.

Woodruff Flowering plants belonging to the bedstraw family. The most common is the sweet woodruff. It has loose clusters of tiny white flowers and its slender leaves are arranged in whorls. The small fruits are covered with hooked bristles.

Wood warbler A greyish-green warbler which is a common summer visitor. It lives in beech, oak and pine forests, spending its life mostly in the tops of trees but building its nest on the ground. Its song is a quivering trill.

Wood warbler

Wood wasp A small group of insects that are more closely related to sawflies than wasps. They are also known as horntails because of the female's tough long ovipositor which sticks out behind her. The female bores into tree bark with the ovipositor to deposit her eggs. The larvae then bore further into the tree.

Woodworm The larva or grub of the furniture beetle. The grubs burrow through wood, sometimes reducing it to sawdust. The holes seen in old timber and furniture are made when the adult beetle bores its way out.

Woolly bear See STINK BUG.

Worm A name given to a wide range of long slender animals without legs. They belong to many different groups. Earthworms belong to the group known as annelids or ringed worms, because their bodies are made up of lots of rings or segments. Silk worms and slow worms are not really worms at all: one is a caterpillar and the other a legless lizard. (See also NEMATODE.)

Woundwort Several species of flowering plant related to the deadnettle. One of the most common species is the hedge woundwort which has softly hairy, heart-shaped leaves and a tall spike of beetroot-coloured flowers. It is a common hedgerow plant. Other species have pink or yellow flowers. The leaves were once used for dressing wounds.

Wrack Member of a group of large brown seaweeds with flat, branched fronds. They are usually found in great numbers on rocky shores. Bladder wrack is a common species. Its fronds bear 'bubbles' or air-bladders which keep the plant buoyant when the tide is in.

Wrasse Member of a group of small thick-lipped fishes, found mostly in shallow water off rocky coasts. Many of them are brightly coloured, the colouring often varying between male and female, and also according to the time of year. There are many species. Some, such as the rainbow wrasse, start life as females, and turn into males later.

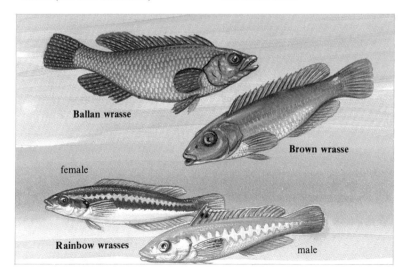

Ballan wrasse

Brown wrasse

female

Rainbow wrasses

male

Wren A tiny brown bird which nearly always keeps its tail cocked up as it scuttles through the undergrowth. Wrens hunt for insects on the ground or in bark crevices, but otherwise hide in hedges and bushes. They build globe-shaped nests. The European wren is one of a family of 59 birds, the rest of which live in the Americas.

Wren

Wryneck A close relative of the woodpeckers that is a summer visitor to most of Europe. It is a mottled brown bird that gets its name from its ability to twist its neck right around. Unlike the woodpeckers it does not have a long sharp beak, nor the habit of chiselling into wood. Instead it nests in existing holes. Wrynecks creep up trees in search of insects and also feed on the ground.

Y

Yaffle See GREEN WOODPECKER.

Yarrow An aromatic flowering plant belonging to the daisy family and commonly found in grasslands. It has flat-topped clusters of white or pink flowers, and its short, finely-segmented leaves give the plant a feathery appearance.

Yeast A group of single-celled fungi that are important in brewing and baking because (feeding on sugars) they form alcohol and the gas carbon dioxide. The chemical process involved is called fermentation.

Yellow archangel An aromatic flowering plant also called the yellow dead-nettle. It has whorls of yellow flowers arranged around the base of the leaves, and the petals are streaked with red. It is a creeping plant with long runners, and is found in woodlands.

Yellow-bellied toad A toad found in much of central and southern Europe. It spends most of the time in shallow water. The brightly coloured belly warns enemies that the toad is not good to eat. The similar fire-bellied toad has red patches on its belly. It is found further north.

Yellowcress Several species of flowering plant closely related to the watercress. The creeping and great yellowcress are the most common species and are found in damp ground. They both bear tiny yellow four-petalled flowers. The great yellowcress is an erect plant whereas the creeping yellowcress is a straggler.

Yellow flag A member of the iris family, otherwise known as the yellow iris. It has sword-shaped leaves and large, showy, bright yellow flowers. The plant is commonly found in wet ground, particularly by ponds and streams.

Yellowhammer The most common of the buntings. Yellowhammers are predominantly yellow birds with darker streaks; females are duller than the males. They are easily detected by their song which sounds like 'a little bit of bread and no cheese'. The birds live in hedgerows and scrub in Europe all year, those in the extreme north migrating south in winter. They eat insects in summer and seeds in winter.

male

female

Yellowhammers

Yellow rattle A semi-parasitic flowering plant belonging to the figwort family. It has fine-toothed leaves ranged in pairs up the stem, and a loose, leafy cluster of yellow two-lipped flowers. It gets its name from the way the ripe seeds rattle inside the inflated fruits. The plant is usually found in grassy places.

Yellow shell moth A common European moth of hedgerows and gardens, often found sheltering beneath leaves. The yellow shell is yellow to brown in colour, with darker bands across the wings.

Yellow-staining mushroom A white toadstool whose cap and stalk, especially at the base, turn bright yellow when cut. The toadstool is poisonous and is found in woods and shrubby places.

Yellow-tail moth Also known as gold-tail, this white moth gets its name from the tuft of golden hair at the end of its abdomen. The female uses the hairs to cover her eggs. Yellow-tail caterpillars are black with white spots and a red stripe along the back, and they feed on various trees.

Yellow-wort A flowering plant related to the gentian and centaury. It grows in fields and meadows on chalky soils, and has loose clusters of yellow flowers. Some of its leaves are borne in opposite pairs and are joined around the stem; others form a basal rosette.

Yew A coniferous tree widely found throughout Europe and commonly planted as an ornament, particularly in churchyards. It grows to a height of 25 metres, with spreading branches. The poisonous seeds are borne singly in bright red, berry-like cups instead of cones. The soft leathery needles are also poisonous.

Yew

Z

Zander A freshwater fish also known as the pike-perch, belonging to the perch family. It grows up to 1 metre long and has many teeth. Zanders eat most other kinds of fishes.

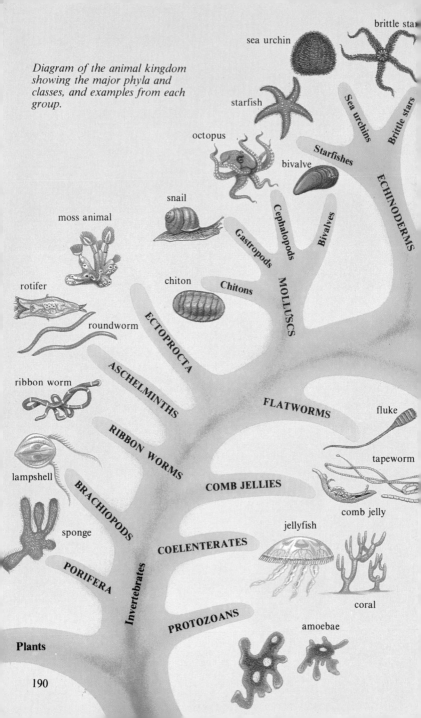

Diagram of the animal kingdom showing the major phyla and classes, and examples from each group.

brittle star

sea urchin

starfish

octopus

bivalve

snail

moss animal

rotifer

chiton

roundworm

ribbon worm

lampshell

fluke

tapeworm

comb jelly

jellyfish

sponge

coral

amoebae

Sea urchins

Brittle stars

Starfishes

ECHINODERMS

Cephalopods

Bivalves

Gastropods

MOLLUSCS

Chitons

ECTOPROCTA

ASCHELMINTHS

FLATWORMS

RIBBON WORMS

COMB JELLIES

BRACHIOPODS

COELENTERATES

PORIFERA

Invertebrates

PROTOZOANS

Plants

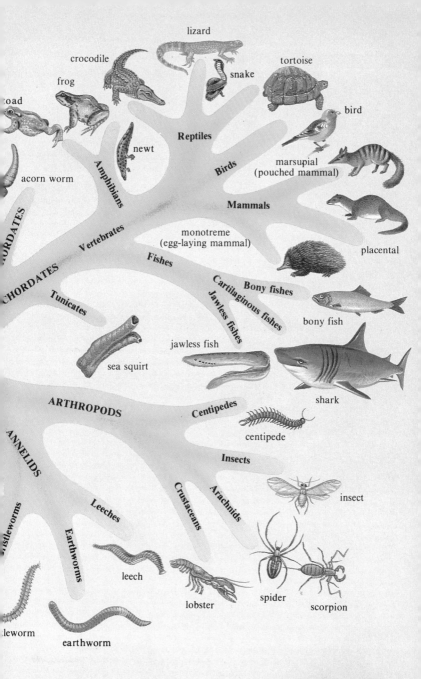

lizard

crocodile

snake

frog

tortoise

bird

toad

Reptiles

newt

marsupial
(pouched mammal)

acorn worm

Amphibians

Birds

CHORDATES

Mammals

Vertebrates

monotreme
(egg-laying mammal)

placental

CHORDATES

Fishes

Bony fishes

Tunicates

Cartilaginous fishes

Jawless fishes

bony fish

jawless fish

sea squirt

shark

ARTHROPODS

Centipedes

centipede

ANNELIDS

Insects

Crustaceans

Arachnids

insect

istleworms

Leeches

Earthworms

leech

lobster

spider

scorpion

leworm

earthworm

191

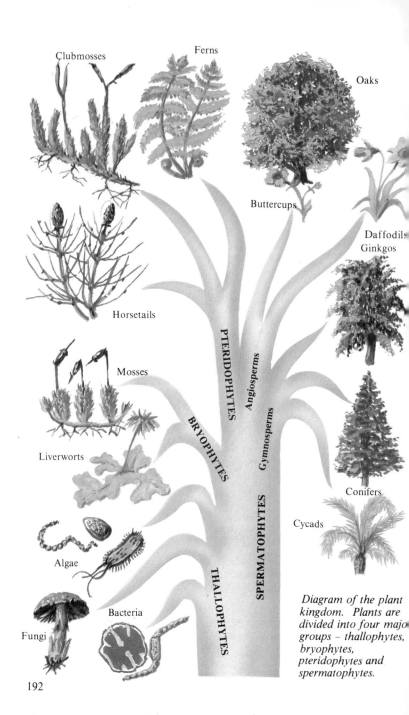

Clubmosses

Ferns

Oaks

Buttercups

Daffodils
Ginkgos

Horsetails

PTERIDOPHYTES

Angiosperms

Mosses

BRYOPHYTES

Gymnosperms

Liverworts

Algae

SPERMATOPHYTES

Conifers

Cycads

THALLOPHYTES

Bacteria

Fungi

Diagram of the plant kingdom. Plants are divided into four major groups – thallophytes, bryophytes, pteridophytes and spermatophytes.